OUTDOOR PURSU

Ian Lockren

Blackie

OUTDOOR PURSUITS

ISBN 0 216 92384 0
First published 1988
© Ian Lockren 1988

All rights reserved. This book is copyright material but permission is given for certain pages to be copied by purchasers, provided that the copies so made are used solely in the purchasing institution. The pages concerned are: the end-of-chapter Worksheets and Exercises 9 and 10 in Chapter 2. No other part of this book may be reproduced, stored in a retrieval system or transmitted in any form or by any means, electronic, mechanical, photocopying or otherwise without prior written permission from the Publisher.

Illustrated by Bill Wilson
Cartoons by Pavely Arts

Published by Blackie and Son Ltd
Bishopbriggs, Glasgow G64 2NZ
7 Leicester Place, London WC2H 7BP

British Library Cataloguing in Publication Data
Lockren, Ian
  Outdoor pursuits.
  1. Great Britain. Outdoor life—Manuals
  I. Title
  796.5′0941
  ISBN 0-216-92384-0

Filmset by Advanced Filmsetters (Glasgow) Ltd
Printed in Great Britain by
Thomson Litho Limited, East Kilbride, Scotland.

ACKNOWLEDGMENTS

The Author and Publishers wish to thank the following for supplying and granting permission to reproduce photographs.

Abbot Hall Art Gallery, Kendal (p. 84)
Allcord Ltd (p. 92)
Steve Ashton (p. 11, p. 24, p. 25, p. 29, p. 91, p. 93 left, p. 97)
Batchelors Ltd (p. 56)
BBC Hulton Picture Library (p. 83)
John Beatty (p. 96)
Bendcrete Climbing Walls (p. 88, p. 93 right)
Canoeist magazine (p. 114)
The Countryside Commission (p. 60)
EPIgas International Ltd (p. 49 top)
PW Gould (p. 102)
Douglas Johnston (p. 111)
Karrimor International Ltd (p. 30, p. 50 right and left)
Kenneth Keane (p. 36)
Optimus International Ltd (p. 49 bottom)
Silva (UK) Ltd (p. 13, p. 66)
Swiss National Tourist Office (p. 36)
Ultimate Equipment Ltd (p. 47)
Ultrasport (p. 77 top left)
Vango (Scotland) Ltd (p. 46)
Wild Water (p.118, p. 119, p. 121)

Cover photograph: Peter Higgins, Benmore Centre, Dunoon, Argyll

INTRODUCTION

Outdoor Pursuits covers a wide range of activities. This book brings together the main areas which are suitable for study by schools, colleges and other groups. There are chapters on each of the following areas:

map and compass work
mountain walking
camping and expeditions
orienteering
rock climbing
canoeing

In addition, there are Appendices to cover the two important general areas of first aid and conservation of the countryside.

All six Chapters follow an identical pattern. Each begins with an Equipment List followed by an Introduction which describes the activity and explains how it will be tackled. The Chapter is then divided into five Sections.

Sections 1, 2 and 3 contain the bulk of the work, information and practical exercises. These Sections are further divided up into sub-sections, which are designed to be tackled in the order in which they have been written.

Chapters 4, 5 and 6 deal with particular sports, and so Section 1 in each is devoted to developing the historical background of the sport as well as providing a fundamental level of knowledge. Section 2 is concerned with the basic skills, and Section 3 takes the student to more advanced levels.

At the end of each Chapter there are a Further Information section and a Worksheet. The Further Information section provides the addresses needed to initiate contact with governing bodies/organisations. The Worksheet contains questions which relate specifically to the Chapter and increase with difficulty as follows:

Questions 1–10 require single sentence answers
Questions 11–17 require multi-sentence answers
Questions 18, 19 and 20 together form a single essay in all but the first and third Chapters, where there are exam-type questions requiring longer answers.

GUIDELINES FOR THE TEACHER/INSTRUCTOR ON EACH AREA OF WORK

Each area of work is *modular* in structure and is designed for use in a two-year course. However the modules, whether considered collectively or individually, will be useful in the whole sphere of outdoor pursuits in education, from one-off lessons and options in the PE curriculum through to GCSE examinations in PE and Outdoor Pursuits, CPVE, TVEI, BTEC and City and Guilds-type courses.

A General Word on Safety

Outdoor pursuits are hazardous by the very nature of the environment or the activities themselves, and so learning and fully understanding about safety aspects is regarded as a pre-condition for participation in all the areas covered by this book.

The modular structure of each Chapter sets out to avoid one of the real dangers of outdoor pursuits in education—that of teaching too much too soon. There have been situations where this 'rush to activity' has led to overconfidence by staff and students alike, with sometimes fatal results. To avoid this, students should never be placed in situations they are not fully-equipped to deal with. Interesting and challenging exercises at every level of learning are included in the text. For minimum safety standards the following publication should be read in conjunction with this book: *DES Safety Series No. 1: Safety in Outdoor Pursuits* (HMSO).

About Each Chapter

Chapter 1   Map and Compass
All work in this Chapter (and in all Sections of the book dealing with maps) is based on two Ordnance Survey 1:50 000 (Landranger) maps: Snowdon and the surrounding area (Sheet 115) and your own local OS map.

It is recommended that the cheapest Silva compass—Type 7NL—be used. This Chapter establishes a basic vocabulary of knowledge which is used throughout the book.

Chapter 2   Mountain Walking
Mountain safety, walking skills and planning are introduced to prepare the student for single-day ventures.

Chapter 3   Camping and Expeditions
Mountain skills are further developed to enable lightweight camping and backpacking expeditions to be undertaken.

Chapter 4   Orienteering
The way students are introduced to this sport is important. A simple case of 'Here's a map and compass, there's the forest!' is totally off-putting. The 'treasure hunt' syndrome also creates feelings of failure all too easily. The intention of this Chapter is to ease students into the sport and encourage links and involvement with local clubs. Orienteering is great fun, providing it is introduced the right way.

Chapter 5   Rock Climbing
The aim of this Chapter is to establish good climbing habits so that this potentially hazardous pursuit can be turned into one of the safest. The emphasis is on developing climbing as a *skill* rather than an activity. The graded progressions outlined in the Chapter should be followed and learning at all levels should be as controlled as possible. For much of the work, reference to a guidebook of a local or often-visited crag is required.

Chapter 6   Canoeing
Students must be able to swim and be comfortable and confident in the water to undertake any water-based course. The theme for the activity is 'enjoyment'. The practical work is concerned specifically with kayak canoeing, although Canadian canoeing is mentioned in the text and recognised as a developing aspect of the sport in this country. All the basic work is directed towards swimming pools and placid water. For some of the practical exercises the following BCU publication is required: *Guide to the Waterways of the British Isles* (British Canoe Union, Surrey).

The Appendices
First Aid and Conservation of the Countryside are themes which are applicable to every aspect of Outdoor Pursuits. The information is intended to act as starting points for further work and experience.

Note
Copyright has been waived in certain sections of this book to allow teachers to photocopy text without fee, for use in the institution by which the book is bought. The sections applicable are:
The end-of-chapter Worksheets
Exercises 9 and 10 in Chapter 2

CONTENTS

1. MAP AND COMPASS — 6
2. MOUNTAIN WALKING — 22
3. CAMPING AND EXPEDITIONS — 44
4. ORIENTEERING — 63
5. AN INTRODUCTION TO ROCK CLIMBING — 82
6. CANOEING — 106

APPENDIX A. FIRST AID — 138

APPENDIX B. THE COUNTRYSIDE AND CONSERVATION — 142

INDEX — 144

1 MAP AND COMPASS

Equipment List

Mountain map–Ordnance Survey 1:50 000 Landranger, Sheet 115. Snowdon and Surrounding Area

Local map–Ordnance Survey 1:50 000 of local area

Silva compass (7NL)

Ruler–30 centimetre

Pencil

Atlas of Britain

Introduction

Map reading and knowing how to use a compass are two of the most important skills in Outdoor Pursuits. Without doubt both should be learnt before venturing into the mountains for walking, climbing or camping expeditions, and a knowledge of them is also necessary to take part in the sport of orienteering and also aspects of river, lake and sea canoeing.

Learning how to use a map and compass correctly is a lot easier than you may think. Don't be put off by them! Remember that a map is a friend with all the information you will need on it. Just like a book, it is there to be read; and a compass is a simple instrument which always points northwards. Put the two together in the ways described in this chapter and you will be able to find your way anywhere.

1 MAPS

1.1 What is a map?

A map is a very accurate picture of a piece of land, based on a photograph taken from the air. It is a 'bird's-eye view' of the land. Like a photograph, it shows everything a lot smaller than it really is. However, unlike photographs, maps do not show the actual mountains, forests, water features, etc. themselves—there isn't enough room. Instead, they use special symbols to represent the features of the land. Map makers try to make their symbols resemble the real thing as much as possible, so water features are coloured blue, forests are green, and so on.

The most popular maps in Britain are made by the Ordnance Survey (called OS for short). The OS have been making maps since 1791, originally for use by the army. They are very useful for finding out more about the mountains or your local area when you go walking, climbing and camping. The two maps on your equipment list are packed with valuable information. To find out some of this, you don't even have to open them out! Let's look at the mountain map first. What does it tell you?

Exercise 1
Locate your local OS map number on the index shown on the back of the map. Which part of the country is it? Use your atlas to find out more.

Exercise 2
Use your atlas again to find out about the part of the country your mountain map covers. What part of Wales is it? Is it near the sea?

Exercise 3
Next, open up and spread out your mountain map. Turn it round, try to get an overall picture of the land it shows. Answer these following questions.
  (i) Where are the highest mountains? Where are the main rivers? (Remember rivers always flow downhill into lakes or the sea.)
  (ii) Where are the towns? Are they in the mountains or on the coast by the sea? Why is this?
  (iii) Do the roads and railways go over the mountains or down the valleys?
  (iv) Draw a simple picture of your map (similar to the one on the back cover of the map) to show these main features, including the coastline.

Mountain map

1.2 The scale of the map

As we have already found out, to fit onto a map, everything has had to be reduced in size—it has been **scaled down**. The **scale** of a map indicates the relationship between distances on the map to distances on the land. Your map scale of 1:50 000 means that everything has been made 50 000 times smaller. For example, if a path on your map is one centimetre in length, this means it is really 50 000 centimetres (or 500 metres) long on the land.

As you have probably now realised, knowing about scale is useful to us. We can, for example, measure how far away a mountain summit is on a map and then work out exactly how far it is in reality. But before looking at how to do this, you need to know that there are other scales which maps can be drawn to. Not all maps have a scale of 1:50 000.

Different map scales can sometimes be confusing and offputting, but for mountain map reading there is only one other map scale which you need to remember. This is the OS 1:25 000 map. On this map, a one centimetre path would really be 25 000 centimetres (250 metres). In other words, a 1:25 000 map is twice as big in scale as 1:50 000 map. This means that more detail about the land can be put in.

MAP AND COMPASS

The two map extracts which follow show the same area of land from your mountain map—an area around a mountain called Tryfan. Notice how much more rugged the mountain looks on the larger-scale map. If you ever climb Tryfan, you will enjoy scrambling through, up and over the rocks around the summit. Paths, bridges, fords and field boundaries, too, are clearer on the larger scale, and for this reason the OS recommends 1:25 000 maps for mountains. Most mountain areas are covered by this scale in a series called *Outdoor Leisure Maps.* Another name for OS 1:25 000 maps is *Pathfinder.* However, not all areas of Britain are as yet covered by this series—it will be 1990 before the 1376 sheets for the whole country are finished.

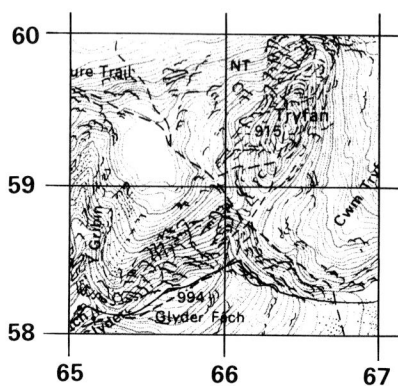

Tryfan as shown on a 1:50 000 map. Note the loss of detail

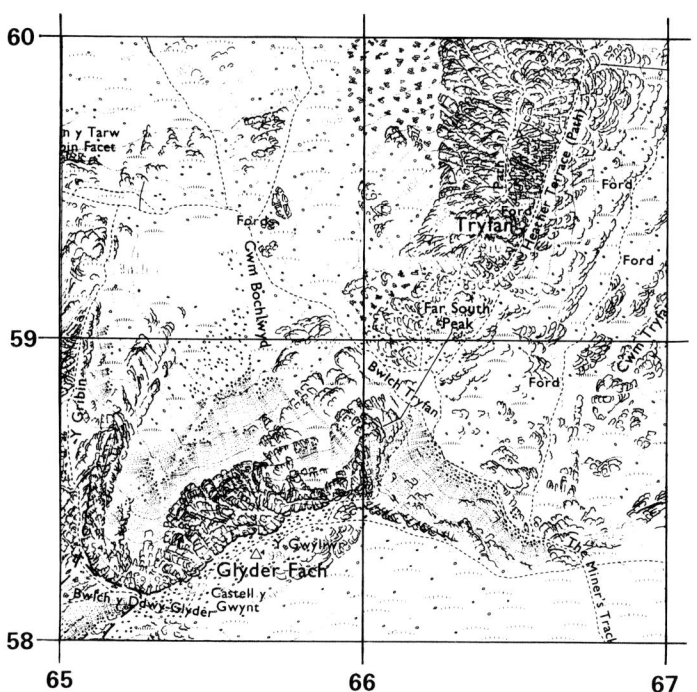

The area around Tryfan, as shown on a 1:25 000 map

We can change 1:50 000 and 1:25 000 map scales into kilometres in the following way.

1:50 000 means that 1 cm on the map = 50 000 cm on the ground

i.e. 1 cm on the map = 500 m on the ground

Now multiplying by **2**: 1 cm × 2 on map = 500 m × 2 on ground

Therefore, 2 cm on map = 1000 m on ground
= 1 km on ground

So 2 cm on the map measures 1 km on the ground.

Similarly for a 1:25 000 map:

1:25 000 means that 1 cm on the map = 25 000 cm on the ground

i.e. 1 cm on the map = 250 m on the ground

Now multiplying by **4**: 1 cm × 4 on map = 250 m × 4 on ground

Therefore, 4 cm on the map = 1000 m on ground
= 1 km on ground

So 4 cm on the map measures 1 km on the ground.

Exercise 4
How far are these distances on your 1:50 000 mountain map: 10 mm, 20 mm, 100 mm (10 cm)?

Exercise 5
Use your map and a ruler to find out how far it is in a straight line between:
  (i) Snowdon and Pen Y Pass Youth Hostel.
  (ii) One roundabout on the Menai bridge road to the other.
  (iii) The 'L' in Llandudno to Conway Castle.

1.3 Signs

It is not necessary to learn all the symbols, lines or colours on a map because they can always be found on the side of the map. However, it is important to get to know a few of them. The most useful sign for the mountaineer is the **contour line**. Contour lines are brown lines which join together points of equal height. If there are a lot of contour lines close together, it means that there is a steep slope and that the land is hilly or mountainous. Also, get to know the difference between a **path** and lines marking **boundaries**—if you confuse these while walking in the mountains, you could walk off the top of a cliff! ('Cliffs' are called crags by mountaineers.)

Exercise 6
Draw and learn the following signs.
Tourist information: telephone, youth hostel
Water features: marsh, lake, footbridge
General features: wood, pipeline, electricity lines
Heights: contour, spot heights
Rock features: outcrop, cliff (crag), scree
All paths

1.4 Grid references

It is very useful and sometimes very important to be able to pin-point a particular place on a map. For example, suppose there was an accident near a small lake close to Snowdon and you had to send for a mountain rescue team. You have your map. How would you describe the lake? There are several in the area. In order to be able to give precise locations all OS maps contain blue lines. These are called **grid lines** and are drawn up and down and from side to side. Where each line meets the edge of the map there is a number, and it is these numbers which help to pin-point a particular location.

For example, the summit of Snowdon lies in a square bounded by grid lines 60 and 61 (along the bottom of your map) and grid lines 54 and 55 (up the side of your map). Therefore a **4-figure grid reference** for Snowdon would be 60 54. Note you do not need to give the numbers 61 or 55, and you always say the grid number along the bottom first. The number up the side then follows. To help you remember this think 'You go *along* the hall before going *up* the stairs'.

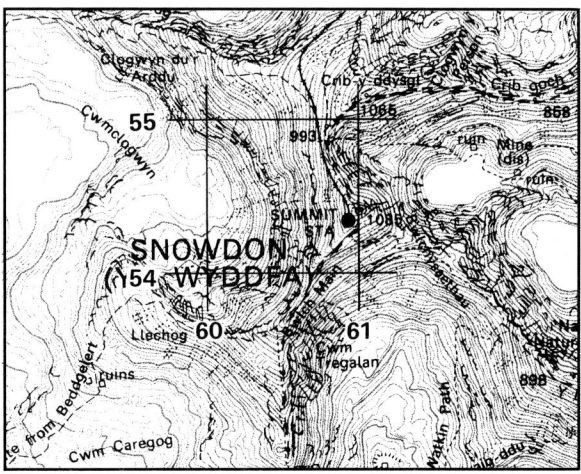

The summit's 4-figure reference is 6054

However, 4-figure references still leave us a whole square in which we have to locate our lake—quite a large area! To get the precise point within this square, imagine that the square is further divided up into *tenths*, as shown below.

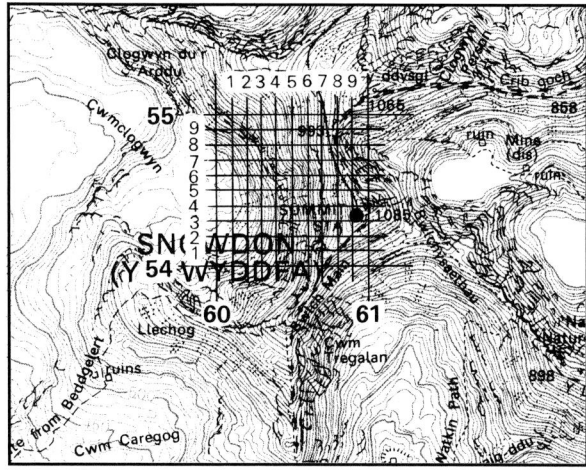

The summit's 6-figure reference is 609 543

The summit station on Snowdon (the red blob) is now 60 and 9 tenths along towards line 61; and 54 and 3 tenths up towards line 55. The **6-figure grid reference** for the summit station is therefore 609 543. The grid reference for the lake in that square is 600 546.

Exercise 7
Find out what is at these grid references:
647 556   610 520   640 545
631 566   634 525

Exercise 8
Give the 6-figure grid references for the following:
The 'S' in Snowdon
Any mountain rescue post
Any lake   Any telephone

1.5 The height and shape of land

Knowing the height and being able to work out the shape of the land from a map are both very important to mountaineers.

Finding the height

The height of land is measured upwards from the level of the sea. So if a mountain summit on a map is given as 1085 (Snowdon), it means that it is 1085 metres above sea-level.

The map is flat but land is not, so changes in height are shown by four symbols:
1 contour lines
2 cliffs (crags) which show that the land is too steep for contours
3 spot heights
4 triangulation pillars (trig points)

The last two give the *exact* height above sea-level at a particular point.

Working out the shape

You can use the information given by the four symbols showing height to work out the shape of a piece of land. In other words, you are able to imagine what the land actually looks like from your flat map. This is an important skill and one that can be easily learnt.

The best help comes from the pattern of contour lines. These are faint brown lines which show that the land along each individual line is the same height above sea-level. Pick a contour from anywhere on your mountain map. Follow it with your finger. The land along the line you are tracing is all at the same height. You may come across a figure written in brown. This figure gives the height above sea-level that is represented by your contour line.

Contour lines represent a difference of ten metres in vertical height. There is a thicker brown line every 50 m.

Follow a contour line as before until you find out its height above sea-level. Now turn the map round so that the height is written the right way up. Find the next contour up. If you were walking from the first to the second contour you would have climbed a height of 10 m on land. If you then walk to where the next contour line is, that is another 10 m of height gained. So far, you have risen 20 m.

> *Exercise 9*
> Locate the nearest contour to the A5(T) road at grid reference 705 597. Imagine you are walking from the road to the cairn (pile of stones) at 705 608. Count the contours you cross and work out how many metres you have gained in height.

As well as giving you the height above sea-level, contours also show how steep the land is. The steepness is shown by the space between the contours. All you need to remember are three patterns of spacings.

1 If lines are close together, the land is steep—the closer together they are, the steeper the land is.

2 If lines are wide apart, the slope is gentle—the wider the contours, the flatter the land.

3 If lines change from being quite close together to being far apart, the land is hilly—called **undulating** land.

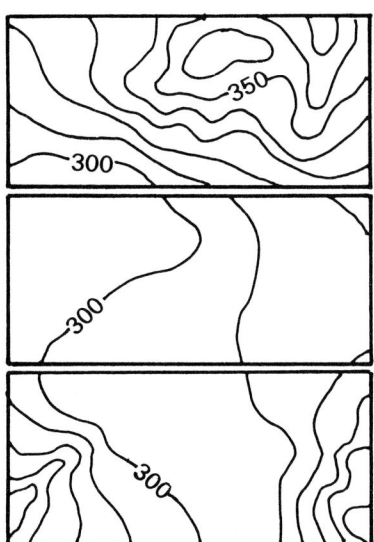

Therefore, simply remember that the closer together contours are, the steeper the land is; the wider apart, the flatter the land is.

Uphill or down?
Sometimes it is difficult to tell if the slope is going uphill or downhill. The following two points will help you to decide.
1 The brown contour height numbers are given so that they read *facing uphill*.
2 If the land has a river close by, the slopes each side of the river are uphill. The river flows downhill, joining bigger rivers, a lake or the sea.

Finding features
As well as showing the height and steepness of land, contours help to identify features of the land such as:
Valleys — long, sometimes narrow land running between higher land
Ridges — long, thin, sometimes knife-edged lines of high land which often lead up to the summits of mountains
Mountain passes — a low point between two summits

The ridges from the summits of Tryfan and Glyder Fach meet, forming a pass

MAP AND COMPASS

Exercise 10
Using your mountain map, a pencil and ruler, draw a straight line from the hotel at 660 558 to the spot height at 667 540.
(i) Are you walking uphill or down?
(ii) Give two pieces of evidence to support your answer.

1.6 Setting your map

'Setting your map' means simply turning the map round until it faces the same way as the land in front of you. There is no single 'right way' to hold a map—it depends on the direction in which you are travelling at any one time. To learn how to set a map, you will need to go outdoors with your local map.

Exercise 11
Go outside, look round and find a hill, a church or some other really noticeable feature. Then find the feature on the map and line it up with the real thing by turning the map round, if necessary. Now do a check with another feature. Find the feature on the map and look up in the same direction. It should be there if you have done the previous part correctly. If it isn't there, try again!

Exercise 12
Your next task is to go for a map walk in your own area, off the roads if possible. Before you go, work out the route and how far you will walk (using the scale). As you go, set your map every so often to fix your position. Try to work out things that you will meet before you get to them, such as a wood, bridge, steep slope, buildings, road junctions, etc.

2 THE COMPASS

In this Section, we shall look at how and why a compass works. Next to a map, it is your best friend when outdoors. It can help you to locate where you are on a map and assist you to find your way. It is very useful, for example, when there are no easily recognisable features on the land, or when mist comes down. It is true that when lost, we tend to walk in circles. A compass can help you to walk a straight line and head in a particular direction.

2.1 What it is, how it works

If you look at a Silva compass, you will see that it is made up of a strip of metal (called the **needle**) balanced on a pin-point so that it swings around freely. The needle is magnetised and always points to a place called the **magnetic pole**. As you can see from the diagram, the Earth has two magnetic poles: north and south. These are not quite in the same place as the North Pole and South Pole, and nobody knows why, but they are not far from them.

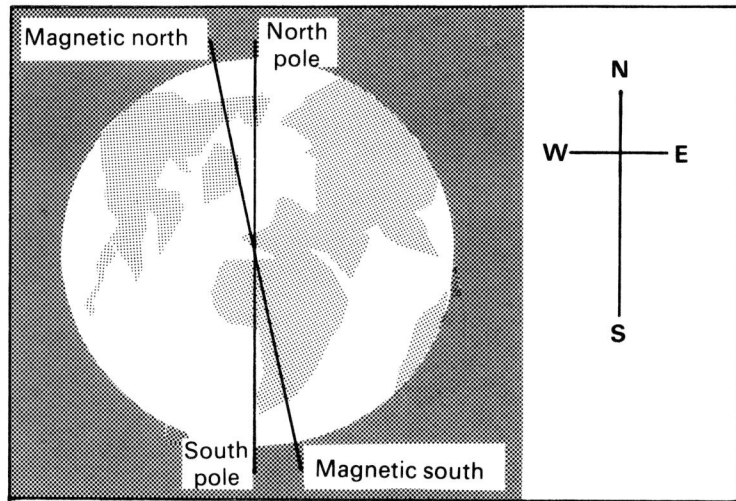

Magnetic poles and points of the compass

In Britain we are closest to magnetic north, so the red end of the needle in your compass points to this. Magnetic north is located somewhere to the north of Canada, and it is not a fixed place. It moves position very slightly every year; again no-one knows why it does this.

How is all this useful? Well, the compass needle tells us which way north is, so we can then also see that the opposite direction is south, and that one side is west and the other east. These are called the **points of the compass**. (To remember which way round west and east are, simply spell **WE**st and the letters themselves tell you!)

However, just knowing where the points of the compass are is not enough for us in the mountains, where the difference between going north and north-west might take you over the edge of a crag! To be more accurate, your compass has been divided up into 360 parts, called **degrees**. The degree marks are given in a circle around the outside of the compass. The N (which stands for north) is 0° and 360°; E (east) is 90°; S (south) is 180° and W (west) is 270°.

Exercise 13
Draw a circle and put on: (i) the points of the compass; (ii) the number of degrees for N, S, E, W.

Exercise 14
Make a simple compass of your own to understand how the device works. You will need a magnet, a needle or piece of wire, some cotton and a drawing pin. Here's how you make your compass.
  (i) Quickly stroke one end of a needle or piece of wire with a magnet a few times in the same direction.
  (ii) Tie the cotton to the middle of the needle and hang it up with a drawing pin.
  (iii) When it stops swinging, the magnetised end will point to magnetic north.

2.2 The Silva compass

In this Section, we will get to know more about the most popular type of compass, the **Silva** compass. Silva is a Swedish company which was established by the Kjellstrom brothers in the 1930s. They make many types of compasses which are light, don't cost much, and are quick and simple to use.

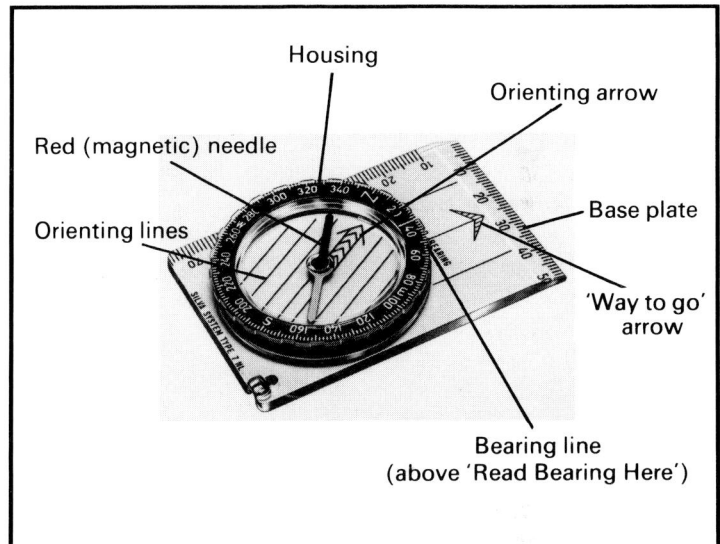

Parts of a Silva compass

A Silva compass has three main parts to it. These are:
1 The **compass** itself. This refers to the magnetised needle, the red end of which is north-seeking. So, when the compass is held flat, it swings round to point to magnetic north.
2 The **housing**. This is the name given to the see-through plastic case around the compass needle, which can be turned with your fingers. When you turn the housing round, the red lines (called **orienting lines**) and the red arrow (called the **orienting arrow**), which are on the bottom of the housing under the needle, also turn round.

MAP AND COMPASS

3 The **base plate**. This is the see-through plastic on which the housing and compass sit. Along the sides of the base plate you will see measurement scales. You can use these as you would a ruler, to measure distances on a map. The most important thing on the base plate is the red arrow at the top. This arrow is called the **direction of travel arrow** for reasons which will become clear later on. Where the arrow meets the housing are the words READ BEARING HERE. This refers to the little black line on the edge of the housing at this point which does not move when you turn the housing round. We will call this the **bearing line**.

2.3 How to set a bearing

A **bearing** is the name given to each of the numbers around the edge of the housing, from 0 to 360 degrees. For example, 120° can be called 'a bearing of 120°'. *Setting a bearing* on your compass means lining your compass up with magnetic north so that you can then find out the direction of any bearing from 0–360°. Setting a bearing involves three easy stages.

1 Turn the housing so that **40** is at the top of the compass in line with the bearing line, as shown in the diagram below.
2 Hold the base plate flat in the palm of your hand with the tail of the base plate square to your body so that the needle swings freely to magnetic north. Be sure that you are not too close to metal (steel fences, doors or even zips) as it can affect the needle of the compass.
3 Now turn yourself round, still holding the compass in your hand until the red orienting arrow (on the bottom of the housing) is directly underneath, and covered by, the red end of the needle. We can call this 'putting the two reds together'. You have now set a bearing of 40°. If you now look along the direction of travel arrow and then look up, everything that you see on this line is on a bearing of 40°. Ensure that the base plate tail is square to your body.

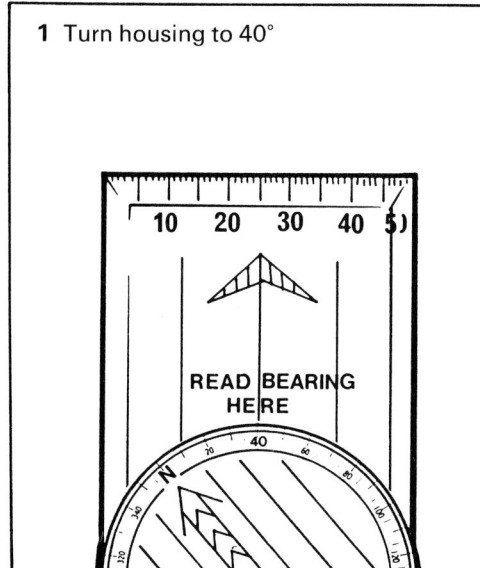

1 Turn housing to 40°

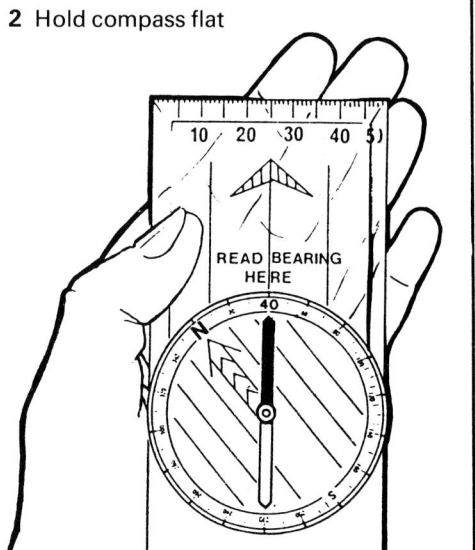

2 Hold compass flat

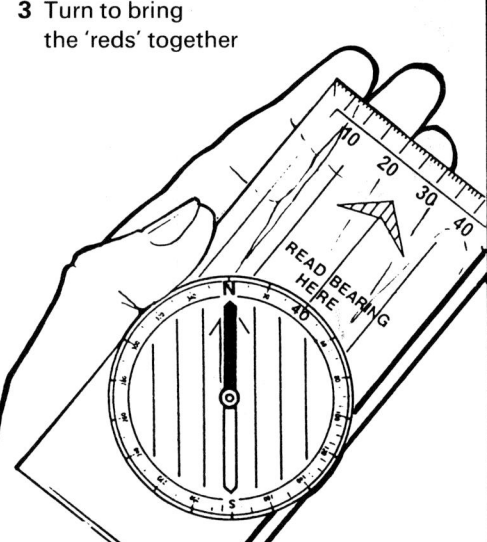

3 Turn to bring the 'reds' together

Exercise 15 Walking a bearing
For this you will need to take your compass outside into the middle of a field or playground. Follow the stages 1 to 3 to set a bearing of 40° again, and then add stages 4 and 5 below.

4. When you have set yourself so that you are looking down the direction of travel arrow, pick a landmark in the distance in line with the arrow. Everything between you and your landmark is along the bearing of 40°.
5. Now, without looking at your compass, walk towards the landmark for about 20 strides. You have now walked a bearing of 40°. Try stages 1 to 5 again, setting and walking bearings of 160°, 220° and 300°.

Exercise 16 Compass treasure hunt
Follow these stages:
1. Place a 10 pence coin at your feet.
2. Set a bearing of 60°.
3. Walk 10 steps towards your landmark and stop.
4. Now set a bearing of 180°.
5. Walk another 10 steps and stop.
6. Then set a final bearing of 300°.
7. Walk 10 steps and stop.
8. Is your money close to your feet?

2.4 Finding a bearing

Once you have learnt how to set and walk a bearing, it is sometimes useful to know how to do it the other way around—to *find* the bearing of a landmark. To do this, you must follow these simple stages:

1. Choose a landmark (or even the corner of the room).
2. Line up the direction of travel arrow with the landmark, holding the compass in front of you on the palm of your hand.
3. Keeping the direction of travel arrow in line with the landmark, turn the housing until the red end of the needle is lined up with the orienting arrow (the two reds are together again!).
4. Read the number above the bearing line; this is the bearing to your landmark.

Exercise 17
Go round your school/college fields, writing down the bearings from one landmark to another, e.g.
School gates to corner of sports hall = 240°
Corner of sports hall to big tree in field = 90°

3 USING A MAP AND COMPASS

Now that you have found out how to read a map and use a compass, the two can be put together to good effect. A map will tell you how far to walk and what you will meet, and a compass will help you to go in a particular direction. When used together, a compass can help you to set your map, find out where on a map you are, and enable you to take a bearing from the map to walk in that direction.

3.1 Grid north and magnetic north—the difference

Before looking at how a map and compass work together, you need to know something that is vital in order to take accurate bearings. We know that a compass needle points to magnetic north. The grid lines on your maps also point northwards, but to a place called **grid north** which is not quite the same as magnetic north.

Why don't grid lines point to magnetic north? The answer is because magnetic north moves its position slightly each year. The difference between the two norths can be seen in the diagram on the next page, and this difference varies from place to place throughout Britain. In the centre of Britain, for example, in 1986, magnetic north was 6° west of grid north; and because magnetic north moves position, this gap will get smaller by 1° in the next six years. In 1992, therefore, it will be 5° west of grid north. The difference always appears on OS maps in the key under the section called **north points**.

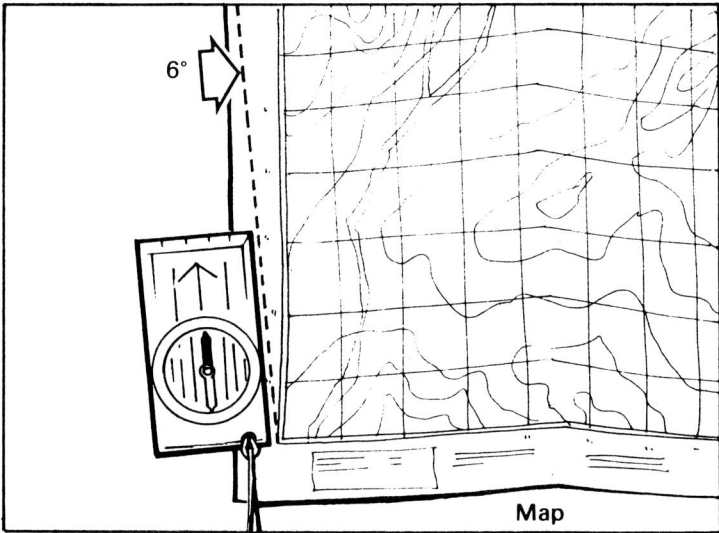

Magnetic north was 6° west of grid north in 1986

> *Exercise 18*
> Check the difference between magnetic north and grid north on both your maps. Is the difference the same for the two maps? If not, why not?

What does this difference mean to us? Well, when we use both a map and a compass, we have to make adjustments to the bearing because the norths they point to are different. The adjustment we make will be whatever the difference is between the two norths as given on the map key. To change a compass bearing to a map bearing, you **subtract** the difference. To change a map bearing to a compass bearing, you **add** the difference. If you are still not quite sure what this means yet, don't worry! All will be explained as you work through this section of the book.

3.2 Setting a map using a compass

You should already know how to set your map by lining it up with features on the land (see Section 1.6). But what happens when you can't see any features—when it's dark, in thick mist or even in a forest? This is where your compass comes in very useful.

You don't know which way grid north is, but your compass tells you where *magnetic* north is, so you have to set your map to point towards magnetic north. To set your local map to magnetic north follow the three stages below, but before you do, find out what the difference is between magnetic and grid north for your area (you should know this from Exercise 18 in Section 3.1).

1 Set the magnetic difference on your compass (e.g. if it's 6°, turn the housing round so that 6° is on the bearing line).
2 Put the compass on your map with the needle pointing towards compass north (the two reds come together).
3 Turn the map under the compass until the blue grid lines are parallel to the orienting lines (the red lines on the bottom of the housing, under the needle).

The map is now **set**. It is good practice to set your map as often as possible.

> *Exercise 19*
> To check this method of setting your local map, go out and try it. When you have set the map, look for features in front of you and see if they are in the right place on the map.

3.3 Locating your position on a map using a compass

So far, we have always assumed that you know where you are on a map. But of course, this is not always the case. In mountainous areas, for example, although you may not be lost, sometimes you will be unsure of your exact position.

To find your position on a map, you need to choose two features on the land that you can also find on your map. Follow the stages below, referring to the diagram as an example.

1. Point your direction of travel arrow at the first of the features—the mountain summit. Find the bearing between you and this feature (get the two reds together, as described in Section 2.4).
2. You now have a compass bearing which needs changing to a map bearing so **subtract** whatever the difference is between the two norths. For example, if the bearing is 66° and the difference is 6°, the map bearing is 60°.
3. Now, place the compass on the map so that a side edge of the base plate is on the mountain summit. Then, keeping this edge on the summit, rotate the compass until the orienting lines are parallel to the grid lines. Also check that the orienting arrow is pointing to the top of the map.
4. Next, draw a pencil line on your map along the base plate edge from the feature. Your position is somewhere along this line.
5. Repeat stages 1–4 for the other feature (the lake edge). Your exact location on the map is at the point where this pencil line crosses the first line.

> *Exercise 20*
> Try this with your local map. Even though you will know where you are on the map, you can still practise the procedure. Instead of using just two features, you can try using three or four.

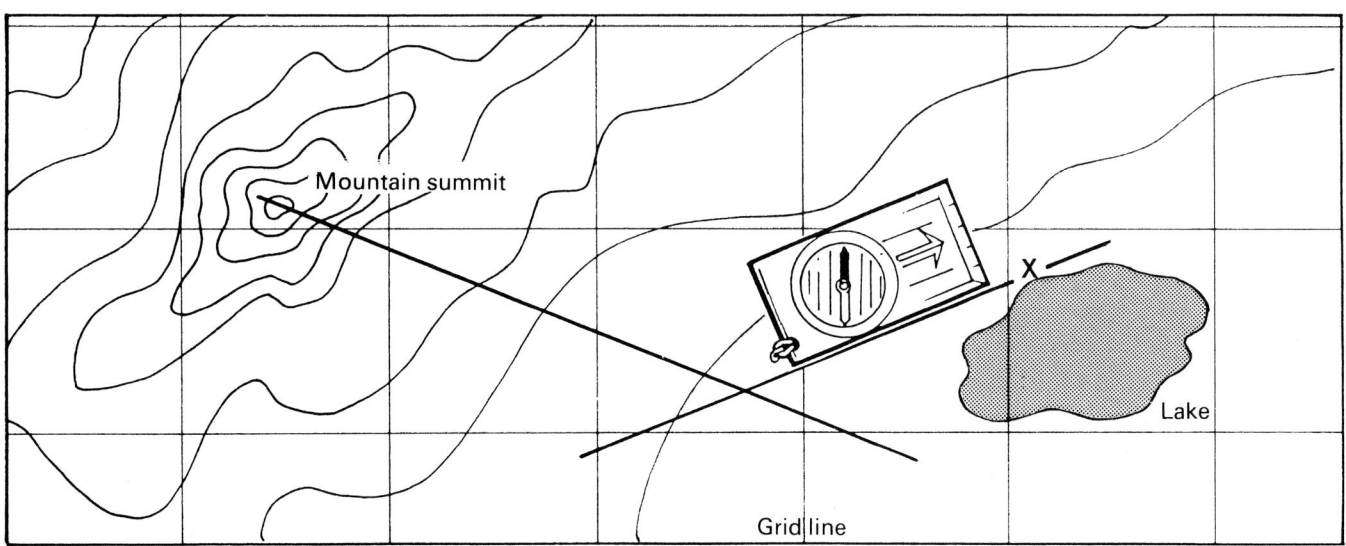

Your position is the point where the two pencil lines cross

MAP AND COMPASS

3.4 Finding a bearing from a map

For us, this is the most important part of map and compass work. It involves knowing where you are on a map and where you want to get to. You could set your map in the way described in Section 3.2 to get a rough idea of the right way to walk; but to be sure you are going in exactly the right direction, it is best to find the bearing from the map, put it on the compass, line it up with a landmark and then walk the bearing. Most of this you know already. So to complete the procedure, this is how to take a compass bearing from a map.

1 Place your compass on the map as shown below with the edge of the base plate along the way you wish to go, and the direction of travel arrow pointing in that direction (not the opposite direction).
2 Turn the housing until the orienting lines are parallel to the grid lines on the map. Make sure the orienting arrow is pointing to the top (north) of the map, not the bottom.
3 Since we are changing a map bearing to a compass bearing, the difference needs to be **added** to the bearing on the bearing line.
4 Now take the compass off the map, hold it in the palm of your hand and turn it round until the two reds are together (the needle and the orienting arrow). Look down the direction of travel arrow, find a landmark in the distance. This is the way to go!

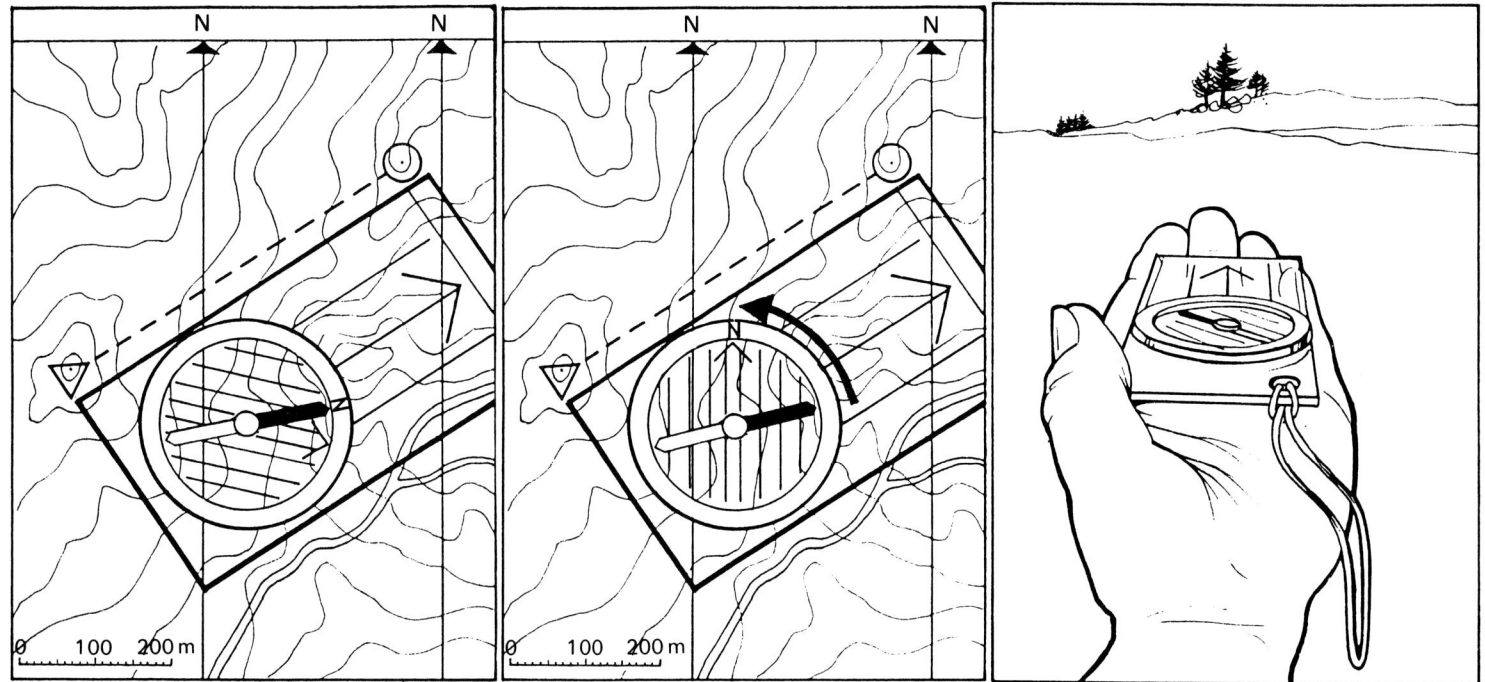

1 *Direction of travel arrow points where you want to go*

2 *Line up the orienting lines with the grid lines*

3 *Choose a landmark*

Exercise 21
Use your mountain map to find the bearings between these grid references:

From GR	To GR	Map bearing	Compass bearing (add the difference)
650 603	662 588		
648 557	625 547		
625 548	608 543		

Conclusion

You now have all the necessary map and compass skills to enable you to venture into the mountains in good weather conditions, and in Chapter 2, that is where we will be going. Remember: read and understand your map and trust your compass.

❓ FURTHER INFORMATION

Maps

For OS maps write to: The London Map Centre, 22 Caxton Street, London SW1H 0QU

For Scotland in particular: Thomas Nelson and Son Ltd, The Edinburgh Map Centre, 51 York Place, Edinburgh EH1 3JD

For other information on OS services the address is: Dept. I.C., Ordnance Survey, Romsey Road, Maybush, Southampton SO9 4DH.

Compasses and equipment

Silva compasses can be bought from most mountain and sports shops but for more information on these and other items of equipment write to: Silva (UK) Ltd, PO Box 15, Feltham, Middlesex TW13 6DF

WORKSHEET

For questions 11–17 you will need your mountain map.

1. What does OS mean?
2. Where does the name 'Silva' come from?
3. What do we mean by the 'two norths'?
4. Give four signs that show the height and shape of land on a map.
5. Explain what has been done to a compass needle if it always points to magnetic north.
6. A Silva compass is made up of three parts. What are they?
7. What differences are there between an OS 1:50 000 and a 1:25 000 map?
8. Why do you think the direction of travel arrow has been given this name?
9. What do we say when the red end of the needle is over the orienting arrow?
10. If you are facing north, which point of the compass is:
    (a) to your left?
    (b) behind you?
    (c) to your right?
11. Describe the land at grid reference 717 655.
12. What signs do you find at the following grid references?
    (a) 747 659 (b) 697 682 (c) 704 675
13. Describe the path between Tryfan (664 594) and Glyder Fach (656 583).
14. Give three reasons why you think the car park at Ogwen (650 603) is a good place from which to begin walking in the mountains.
15. Locate Y Garn (630 595) and use the contours and signs to describe:
    (a) the summit
    (b) the land immediately east of the summit
    (c) the land immediately west of the summit.
16. How far is it in metres in a straight line from Llanberis to Snowdon?
17. Find these three Welsh names and say what you think each means in English.
    (a) Llyn
    (b) Afon
    (c) Nant
18. Give three important uses for a compass.
19. Explain how you would take a bearing from a feature on the land.
20. Explain how to take a bearing from a map and change it to a compass bearing.

© Ian Lockren 1988   Permission is given to photocopy the above worksheet without fee for use in the institution by which the book is bought.

2 MOUNTAIN WALKING

Equipment List

Mountain map

Silva compass

Map measure or string

Rope

1 kg margarine tub

Large polythene bag

Introduction

Mountaineering (also sometimes called mountain climbing) is the name given to walking and climbing activities in the mountains. It also includes rock scrambling. Mountain walking and some scrambling skills are covered in this Chapter; mountain expeditions in the next; and rock climbing in Chapter 5.

Walking, in the form of rambling and hiking, is probably the easiest and most popular recreational pursuit. Mountain walking (sometimes called fell and hill walking) has over the years, for a number of reasons, become one of Britain's fastest growing leisure activities. It can be adventurous, challenging and exciting. But it can also be dangerous, and you have to be well aware of the hazards of the mountains.

Although the British mountains are not nearly as high as, for example, some of those in Europe (and because of this, some people only call them 'hills'), you should not treat them lightly. Always go well prepared and properly equipped. The terrain is rough, the weather can change in a matter of minutes, and the distances involved in walking up and down mountains are that much greater than on the flat. You will get aching legs, blisters, cold, wet and lost at sometime or other. If you are really unlucky, you will get all of them at once!

In this Chapter, we shall look at the skills needed for a day's walk during the late spring, summer and early autumn months. We will also look at how to plan a route and what to do if things do go wrong.

> *Exercise 1*
> Use an atlas to locate and draw a map of the mountain-walking areas of Britain, (south-west, northern and north-west England; central and northern Wales; southern and northern Scotland).
>
> *Exercise 2*
> All the above areas are to the west and north of Britain, where you will find older, harder rocks. Next, find out the names given to each of these areas and also the names of their highest mountains. Make a table like the one below.
>
> | Mountain area of Britain | Name | Highest peak |
> |---|---|---|
> | North Wales | Snowdonia | Snowdon (Yr Wyddfa) |
> | | | |

1 WALKING SKILLS AND EQUIPMENT

This Section introduces you to the things you need to consider on a one-day mountain walking trip, using footpaths and tracks. You should not venture off recognised paths or stay any longer than one day until you have a reasonable amount of mountain environment experience. You can only gain this experience by going to and walking in the mountains.

1.1 Walking uphill

The first thing you will notice is that mountain paths are rough! You need to look where you are putting your feet, and also look at the ground a few paces ahead of you to make sure that it is safe and easy to walk on. Try to put the whole of your foot on the ground, with most of your body weight on your heel. This makes use of the strong muscles in your thigh. Walking on your toes uses the weaker calf muscles, which soon become tired and sore.

The second thing that becomes clear is that walking uphill takes far more energy than walking on the flat. This means that when going uphill, you need to walk more slowly in order to conserve energy. Even if a mountain path is easy to begin with, it is a common mistake to walk too fast and become tired too soon. Keeping to a **steady pace** is vital. It is therefore the same as running a long distance race: if you start out too fast, you have no energy left at the end. When mountain walking, it's important to save energy all the time so that you are never too tired to react to emergencies, or to reach your destination.

You can save energy by keeping to an easy and manageable pace, and you should be able to keep this pace up for long periods. You *waste* energy by putting in sudden bursts of speed followed by slower phases, and having to stop often to recover. Think of your body as being like a car: a car uses less petrol when driven at a constant speed than it does when the speed increases and decreases frequently.

You won't be able to keep up a fast pace for long

MOUNTAIN WALKING

To keep to the same pace, your feet need to hit the ground in a regular rhythm, as if you were a marching soldier. Soldiers often sing to help them walk in a regular rhythm. Thinking about your breath helps, too. For example, you could walk so that you take two steps to each breath. However, you shouldn't be going so fast that you don't have breath to chat to your companions!

What happens when you come to a particularly steep section? Here, you should still try to keep to the same pace. You do this by altering the length of your stride and slowing down, so that although your stride is shorter, your feet are still hitting the ground to the same pace as before. When the path levels off again, lengthen your stride and speed up a little; and on downhill sections, don't be tempted to increase the pace—lengthen your stride instead.

When the ground becomes too steep to keep to the same pace, there are a number of things you can do. First, lean well forward. This helps to keep you moving by making it easier to bring your foot up for the next step. Secondly, go up the path in small zig-zags to help keep your feet flat, so that you don't have to walk on your toes.

Shorten your stride when going uphill

So there are seven points to remember:
1 save energy
2 keep to a steady pace
3 to go slower on steep sections, *shorten* your stride
4 to go quicker on level or downhill sections, *lengthen* your stride
5 lean slightly forward
6 put the whole of your foot on the ground
7 zig-zag on very steep sections

> *Exercise 3*
> Find a hill or steep slope and practise pace setting and shortening and increasing stride lengths to keep to the same pace.

1.2 Stopping for rests

Frequent stopping breaks the pace and rhythm of walking. If you choose an easy and comfortable pace, you will be able to go for long periods without stopping. However, it's a good idea to stop briefly after the first fifteen minutes or so in order to take off any clothes you don't need once your body has warmed up. After this, aim for a ten minute stop each hour, but choose the resting place carefully. For instance, a good place to stop would be at the *top* of a steep section, not before it—you would find it hard to get back into rhythm if a steep section immediately followed your rest. So try to have a level or downhill section in front of you when you intend to stop.

When you do stop, put on extra clothing—a jumper or cagoule—because you will cool down very quickly. Also, have someting to eat. It is important, too, to deal with sore feet: if there is a hint of a blister on your foot, put on a sticking plaster.

It is the leader's responsibility to recognise tiredness, and the pace of the party should be adjusted so that the slowest person can comfortably keep up. However, if someone should complain of exhaustion then, of course, a stop should be made immediately.

> *Exercise 4*
> Using your mountain map find the path called the Pyg Track at grid reference 640 554. The path goes from Pen-y-Pass youth hostel to the summit of Snowdon. Find three good stopping places along the path to the summit—remember to look at the contours to find the steep sections.

1.3 Walking downhill

Many accidents happen on the way downhill because walkers relax too much, don't keep to the paths and become careless. For a number of reasons, descending is sometimes harder work than going up. For one thing, you may be tired; also, going downhill can put strain on your knees and ankles, and this can be painful. The strain is usually caused by overstriding (taking steps that are too long). Try to resist this and keep to a steady pace.

Although it might seem safer to lean back when descending, don't! This gives you no control if your feet slip. Instead, try to lean forward to put all your foot on the ground, and bend your knees. Zig-zag if necessary and, if the ground is soft enough, dig in your heels.

1.4 Walking on different terrains

The type of ground (**terrain**) on a mountain can vary over quite short distances. Often, it will turn into grass, stones, scree or even rocks and boulders. It may become very steep, follow narrow ridges or cross streams. We will consider how to cope with each of these different terrains in turn.

Grass

Short grass is usually nice and easy to walk on. However, it can sometimes be slippery even when dry, and if wet, it becomes dangerous. When descending, dig in your heels, bend your knees and don't run down.

Loose stones

Often, a path becomes so eroded (worn down) by thousands of pairs of feet that it disintegrates into large and small stones. Take care not to dislodge the stones, but if you do, shout 'BELOW' to warn anyone further down the mountainside of the danger.

Scree

A typical scree slope

'Scree' is the name given to steep slopes of loose stones and small rocks. Paths usually avoid scree but it may sometimes be necessary to cross some. Again, be careful

MOUNTAIN WALKING

not to dislodge stones. Scree, however, is usually quite well-packed and doesn't move more than a few centimetres when you walk over it.

A way of descending scree that can be fun but is more dangerous than normal walking is called **scree running**. This can be done on small stones of about ping-pong ball size, and it involves a controlled slide downhill. By leaning back, bending your knees and digging your heels well in, the scree should move down with you. You must make sure that the place where the scree ends is flat and safe.

However, there are not many places left in Britain where scree running can be carried out safely. Many slopes have been worn out by years of use, so that now, only earth is left. For this reason, it is always best to treat screes with respect and only descend them if necessary, in the hope that such well known and loved mountain features remain with us. If you do need to descend scree that is not suitable for running, do so in an 'arrowhead' formation, so that if stones are dislodged, they will not hit anyone lower down. If an arrowhead is not possible, then keep in a line, close together in single file.

Rocks and boulders

Sometimes it will be necessary for you to use your hands as well as your feet when a path goes through, up or over large boulders or small rock faces. This technique is called **scrambling**. It is usually good fun and a welcome change from 'foot slogging'.

Scrambling is a form of **rock climbing**, so be careful and remember that safety lies in good footholds. When moving up, make sure that you move either one arm or one leg at a time—always have *two feet* and *one hand* or *two hands* and *one foot* on the rock face at any one time. Never just hang on by your arms or take away both hands at the same time. Scrambling which requires a safety rope is discussed in Chapter 5.

Ridges and very steep slopes

Walking and scrambling on mountain ridges is often exciting, the views spectacular and the route useful, taking you to one or more summits without the need to gain, then lose and then regain lots of height. But great care is needed, especially when windy.

(a) *Descending wide scree in an arrowhead formation*

(b) *Descending narrow scree in single file*

Crossing small streams

Paths will sometimes take you across mountain streams, but you should only cross deeper streams when the water is fordable (able to be waded through). If possible, keep your boots dry but if there is a chance of getting wet, it's a good idea to take off your socks and cross in boots alone. 'Boulder hopping' is probably the best method of crossing. Try to choose fairly flat boulders.

Crossing large mountain streams, particularly when full, is difficult, but in an emergency it can be done reasonably safely using a rope.

Be careful when 'boulder hopping'!

1.5 What to wear

It is often said that no two mountaineers would agree about what to wear or what equipment to carry, and after gaining some experience, you, too, will have your own preferences. It is a good idea not to spend too much until you know exactly what it is that you want. Early on, however, you will feel the need to get your own boots, waterproofs and rucksack.

Inner clothes

The main function of inner clothing is to trap air between several layers of clothes, so that the warmth of your body is not allowed to escape. Even on a cold day you produce heat, particularly if working hard, such as walking up a mountain. The more layers you wear, the better. For example, two light jumpers will trap more air close to your body than one thicker jumper.

It's a good idea to wear a tee-shirt as well as a shirt and jumper(s), with trousers (but not jeans) tucked into long socks. The material which these items are made from (the **fabric**) is quite important, because some fabrics are warmer than others.

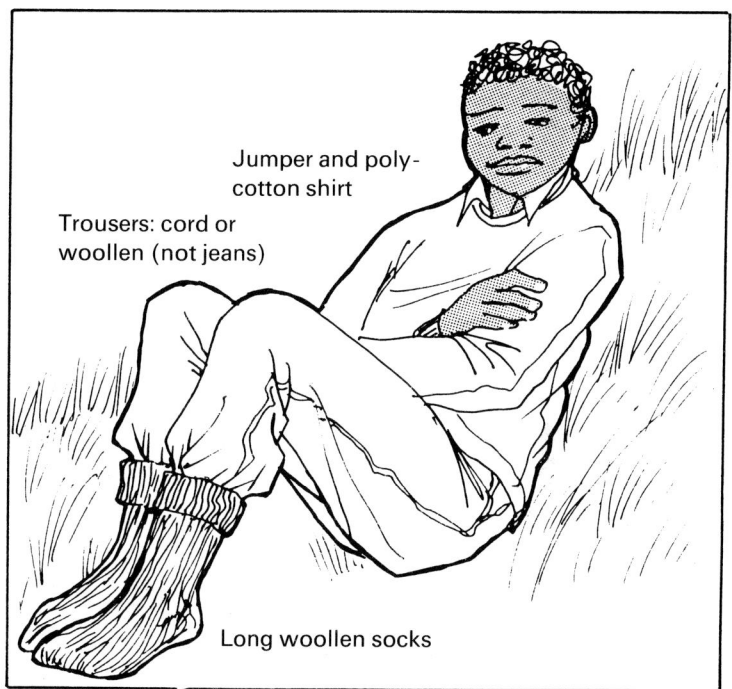

Inner clothes to keep you warm

Fabric made from natural fibres, such as wool and cotton, are loose and have lots of holes and spaces where air can be trapped and warmed by body heat. When wet, the fibres absorb the water and swell up, blocking off some of the holes and spaces making the fabric reasonably waterproof. However, natural fibres take a long time to dry out, and the main problem with this is that when clothes are wet, body heat escapes very quickly. This is why jeans, which are made from cotton, are totally unsuitable for mountain walking.

Fabric made from man-made (**synthetic**) fibres is tighter, thinner and lighter, but it does not trap air nearly as well and so is not as warm as natural fabric. When wet, however, it does not absorb as much water, and so dries off more quickly than clothing made from natural fibres.

Faced with these advantages and disadvantages, what do you wear? Well, if you wear clothes made from cotton or wool and you make sure they don't get wet, then they would certainly be warmer than clothes made from man-made fabric. But you can't guarantee that a cotton tee-shirt, for example, will stay totally dry. It will absorb your body sweat, become damp and then take a long time to dry out. It will not hold in the warm air in this condition, and you will feel cold and uncomfortable when you stop walking or if a wind springs up.

The answer, therefore, would be to wear clothes made from a *mixture* of natural and man-made fibres. To dry off quickly, the fabric should be at least 30% man-made fibre, such as polyester or nylon. A poly-cotton tee-shirt, for example, is light and ideal for summer walking.

Exercise 5
Check your clothes. Is the fabric cotton, synthetic or both? Would it be useful in the mountains? Check at home for suitable trousers, tee-shirts, socks and jumpers.

Outer clothes

Whereas the main function of inner clothes is to keep you warm, the main function of outer clothes is to keep the wind and rain out, to form a barrier so that you are **insulated** from the weather.

Outer clothes include windproof coats (**anoraks**), lightweight, waterproof tops (**cagoules** or 'cags' for short), waterproof **overtrousers** and **boots**. It is also a good idea to wear, or at least to have with you, a hat and gloves. Up to one third of the heat lost from your body can come from your head.

Outer clothes to protect against the weather

Anoraks consist mostly of natural fibres. They are warm, but not particularly waterproof. Cagoules, on the other hand, are usually made from lightweight nylon which has been waterproofed with PVC (polyvinylchloride) on the inside. As well as being waterproof,

WALKING EQUIPMENT

cagoules are, to a certain extent, windproof. Most people wear an anorak until it starts to rain, when they take out their cagoule and put it on top. They take their cagoule off when the rain stops.

You may wonder why people don't simply wear a cagoule all the time, and do without an anorak entirely. The answer is, first, that dry anoraks are warmer than cagoules. Secondly, the natural fibres from which an anorak is made 'breathe' (they let air pass in and out), while artificial fibres, like nylon, do not. The problem with 'non-breatheable' clothing materials is that the perspiration created by your body when you are working hard (e.g. when mountain walking) gets trapped between the material and your body. It cannot escape through the fibres, and so you can get almost as wet from trapped perspiration as from rain. This is why it is always a good idea only to wear a cagoule for as short a time as possible.

Recently, some manufacturers have tried to combine both qualities in a cagoule which is composed of a waterproof material that 'breathes' to some extent. A wide variety of different coatings and non-sweat materials is available for this type of cagoule. Some have millions of tiny holes big enough to allow sweat to pass out but too small to let rain in. However these cagoules are not cheap, and some are not even particularly successful, so for summer walking, when staying warm isn't too much of a problem, lightweight, proofed nylon 'cags' are quite adequate.

Boots

A good pair of boots is important. They have to protect your feet from the rugged terrain and the weather, which means they should be strong, comfortable and waterproof.

Comfort often depends on you looking after your feet, as much as the type of boots you wear. Cut your toenails, put plasters on at the slightest sign of rubbing and wear well-fitting socks. Of the boots themselves, there are two kinds available: heavy and lightweight.

The traditional heavy leather walking boot has remained unchanged for a number of years. It has what is called a **Vibram sole** which is usually glued and screwed to the leather upper of the boot. The advantages of this type of boot are long life, warmth and protection. However there are disadvantages which many people now think outweigh the advantages. Stiff leather is heavy, it has to be 'broken in' and Vibram soles are known to be slippery on wet grass. For these reasons, wearing them has been described by some people as 'walking in a pair of heavy leather coffins'.

New developments in walking boots include the Klets sole

Lightweight boots have been developed in the 1980s. The advantages of these are that they need little or no breaking in, and they are comfortable to wear whilst giving all the protection that is necessary. Many of the most recently developed boots have what is called a **Klets sole**. This sole is made up of shallow, widely-spaced 'lugs' around the edges, similar to the Vibram sole, but with studs in the centre, rather like a soccer boot. This helps to provide grip on wet surfaces.

MOUNTAIN WALKING

There are two types of lightweight boot:
1 lightweight leather, which is long-lasting and waterproof to an extent
2 man-made fibre, which is very lightweight and made from a variety of synthetic materials, including nylon. There are doubts about its waterproof qualities, although new developments are improving this all the time.

For summer mountain walking, then, you need to look for a boot that is comfortable, gives support to your foot and ankle and has either a Vibram or a Klets sole which is not too thin. Therefore a lightweight boot is probably the most suitable.

"THESE WERE LIGHTWEIGHT BOOTS WHEN WE SET OFF!"

1.6 What to carry

You will need, of course, a rucksack in which to put all the things required for a walk in the mountains. The size of rucksack depends on what you will be doing and for how long. We shall consider two types of **day sack**. The first is made from natural material (cotton or canvas) which is usually proofed to stop water getting in. However, as you know, the cotton or canvas exterior will take a long time to dry out after rain. These sacks tend to be heavier than the second type, which are made from nylon. Be aware of very cheap nylon sacks which are not

A good-quality day sack

particularly strong and will have no, or minimal, waterproofing. If you spend some more money you will get a stronger and better proofed sack, which will be much more useful to you. Be careful not to damage the inside surface of the rucksack because this is where the proofing has been applied.

There are many day sacks of these two types in the shops. Which one you buy will depend upon your own particular needs. For example, side pockets are useful and so, too, is the addition of a plastic sleeve at the top of the sack which, as well as protecting the contents from the weather, pulls out to be used in emergency bivouac situations (Section 3.2). If you decide to buy one, here is a useful tip: put all your gear in a polythene bag and then try out different sacks with your load. Also, don't forget to try the rucksack on!

When packing your rucksack, you need to remember the British weather! You cannot rely on it being fine on top of a mountain even if it's warm and dry in the valley. You need to be prepared for the cold and wet. Line your rucksack with a polythene bag to make sure your equipment will be kept dry. Take gloves, a hat, waterproofs, food; and it is essential to pack extra clothes, (socks and a jumper at least). You can always take things off if you get hot but you can't put more clothes on if you haven't got them.

Be prepared for the cold and wet!

The following is a summary of personal equipment:
1 anorak, cagoule and overtrousers
2 warm trousers and socks
3 strong, comfortable lightweight boots
4 lightweight rucksack and polythene liner
5 map, compass, spare clothes, food and water, polythene 'bivy' bag (see Section 3.2), whistle and torch.

A Leader will need to pack all the above plus much more equipment to deal with emergency situations (Section 3). This additional equipment includes: rope, pencil, first-aid kit, sleeping bag, paper, stove, fuel, windproof matches, route card.

Exercise 6
Check your local mountain shop for the variety of waterproofs, rucksacks and boots. What are the differences between cheap and more expensive equipment?

Exercise 7
Assemble a Leader's type of emergency pack for your rucksack from things available at home. Use a small, lightweight container to put everything in (e.g. a 1 kg margarine tub). You need such things as matches, tea bags, sugar, chocolate, pencil, paper, plasters, packet soup.

---

2 ROUTE PLANNING

It is important to know how to plan mountain routes even if you are not intending to lead groups yourself. It is best at this stage to choose routes which keep to paths—there are plenty marked on maps. The first thing to do is to pick a mountain and plan well in advance, at least the day before. Next, you need to work out how long it will take to walk the route. Then it is advisable to write down the route on a **route card**, decide on emergency routes off the mountains and leave a note of your journey with someone in the valley below. This way, if things do go wrong, the rescue teams will know where to look for you. At the end of the day, don't forget to tell the person that you have returned!

Exercise 8
Find grid reference 647 557 on your mountain map. You are beginning a mountain walk from this point. Where could you leave a note of your proposed route?

(Note: It may be difficult to get strangers to take the responsibility of holding details of your route. Leave them with a friend, if possible.)

MOUNTAIN WALKING

2.1 Choice of route

Choosing a suitable route involves four planning stages:
1 Choose your mountain. Try to picture its shape from the contours on the map.
2 Decide on the best place to start from—usually a car park.
3 Using the footpaths, select a route to the summit. Also note possible escape routes off the mountain in case of emergency. (Check them in the local guide book if there is one.) If there are a choice of paths, some useful points to remember are:
   – don't choose a path that appears to go straight to the summit, it's usually steep and difficult. The shortest path is often the hardest and therefore not the quickest.
   – choose a path that takes you to a ridge.
   – try not to use paths that involve losing and gaining a lot of height.
4 Using footpaths, select a route down. Try not to retrace your steps, although this may be unavoidable. Make the descent as easy as possible for yourself.

2.2 Length of route

Once we have decided on a route, how do we find out if it's too long? A simple way is to use a method called **Naismith's rule**. This method, named after a famous Scottish mountaineer, gives an approximate indication of the time it would take an average group to walk in the mountains. It is based on two measurements which you need to get from the map: (1) the *distance* and (2) the amount of *height gained* from start to finish.
  1 *The distance.* Naismith suggested a speed of 4 km per hour for mountain paths. That allows 15 minutes for every 1 km walked. The distance can be worked out using a **map measure** which is a small instrument with a distance dial in various scales. Running the wheel along the route turns the dial, and you can read off the distance by looking at the correct scale. Or you could use a piece of string, laying it along the route and then using the scale on the map to find out the distance. In the diagram below the distance is 5 km. Therefore:

   Time = 5 × 15 = 75 minutes or 1 hour 15 minutes for the distance of 5 km.

   We have to add on another 1 hour 15 minutes to get down again, making a total time of 2 hours 30 minutes. Now we have to add to this the extra time taken to walk uphill.
  2 *The height gained.* Using Naismith's rule, we need to add 15 minutes for every 100 metres climbed. That is 1.5 minutes for every 10 metres (or every uphill contour). From the diagram, we can see that the starting height at the car park is 500 metres above sea-level, and that the height at the summit is 1000 metres. Therefore:

   Height gained 1000 − 500 = 500 metres

The time needed to be added is:

   5 × 15 = 75 minutes or 1 hour 15 minutes for the height of 500 metres.

This 'height time' is then added to the 'distance time':

   Distance time = 2 hours 30 minutes
   Height time   = 1 hour 15 minutes
   Total time   = 3 hours 45 minutes

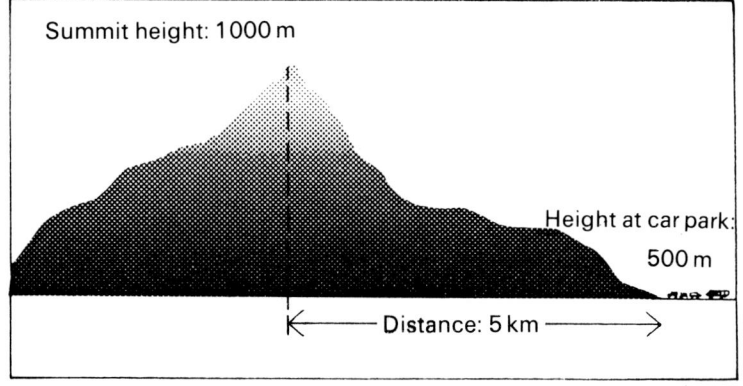

ROUTE PLANNING

Exercise 9

For this exercise let's take an example of a route from your mountain map and work through the four planning stages described above.

1. Choice of mountain: the summit of Snowdon (Yr Wyddfa). Try to picture its shape (the diagram below will help). The summit has the shape of a three-sided pyramid with _____ ridges coming down from it. (*Fill in the blank.*)
2. Starting place: the car park at Pen-y-Pass youth hostel, grid reference 647 557.
3. Choice of route up: there are three possibilities. One, called the Miner's Track, is an easy route for much of the way so we shall use this to return at the end of the day. To go up we shall choose the Pyg Track which goes due _____ from the car park. Follow the path with your finger to get an idea of the route. It starts off fairly easily allowing you to get into a nice steady pace. The first steep section takes us onto a ridge at _____. Here, if the weather is fine, we get a spectacular view of Snowdon. The ridge called Grib _____ is an excellent but difficult ridge route to Snowdon, so we shall leave this for another day and continue beneath it on the Pyg Track, which keeps much of the height we have already gained getting on to the ridge. The next steep section is at 620 548, directly above a _____ _____, then the path levels off following the contours above a small lake called _____. From then on, it is quite a hard walk and scramble to the _____ at 608 549. From here on, the way is easy, following the path next to the mountain railway to the summit.
4. Choice of route down: there are a number of paths back to the car park. The ridge routes include _____–_____ and the eastern ridge, Bwlchysaethau and Y Lliwedd. But for an easy way down, we retrace ourselves for a short distance to the path junction above Glaslyn (61__ 54__) and take the lower path, the Miner's Track, down to the shores of Llyn _____, where it becomes a wide path to the car park.

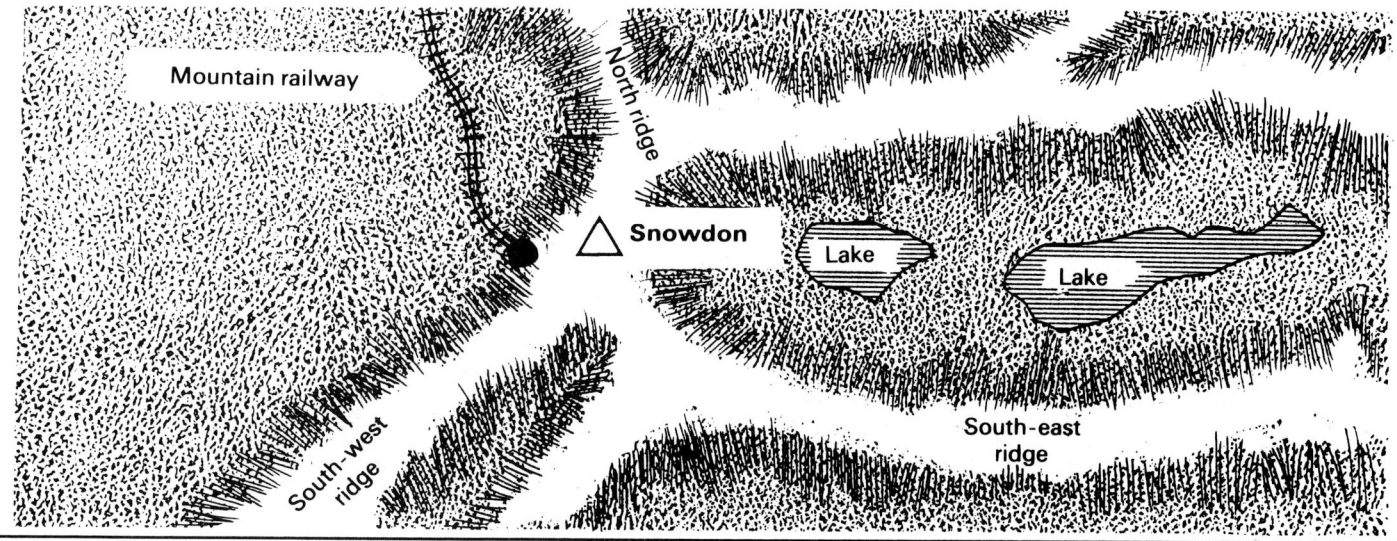

© Ian Lockren 1988   Permission is given to photocopy the above exercise without fee for use in the institution by which this book is bought.

MOUNTAIN WALKING

Exercise 10
Let's now work out the time it would take us to do the Snowdon route. Fill in the blanks.
1. The distance along the path from Pen-y-Pass to the summit is _____.
   Rounding this off to the nearest km gives _____.
   Using Naismith's rule, the time is therefore _____ h _____ min.
2. The height at Pen-y-Pass is _____ m.
   The height at the summit is _____ m.
   The height needed to be gained is therefore _____ m.
   Rounding this up to the nearest metre gives _____ m.
   Using Naismith's rule, the time to be added is _____ h _____ min.

Adding 1 and 2 together gives _____ h _____ min.

Adding 10 minutes per hour for stops gives _____ h _____ min.

Adding 30 minutes for lunch at the summit gives _____ h _____ min.

Now, measure the distance of the return journey via the Miner's Track, work out how long this will take and add it to the time taken to get up to give you an overall time for the walk (you will probably only need one 10 minute rest on the way down). The overall time should be somewhere around 5 hours 30 minutes.

Exercise 11
Plan and walk a route using your local map. Work out how long it will take you. If you are walking on roads a speed of 6 km per hour should be used.

© Ian Lockren 1988 Permission is given to photocopy the above exercise without fee for use in the institution by which this book is bought.

Naismith's rule, however, is only a guide to the time it would take. Extra time should be allowed for poor weather, carrying heavier gear, a particularly slow pace (the pace of the slowest member of the group).

2.3 Escape routes

'Escape routes' are another important consideration in route planning. Don't be tempted to ignore them until you need one. Escape routes are easy ways back down to the valleys from particular places along the route. For example, when walking our Snowdon route, it would be easy to turn round and go back to the car park if the weather changed or if someone had an accident up to about grid reference 625 547.

After this point, the best place to descend would be where the Pyg Track meets the Miner's Track at 615 548, going down to Llyn Llydaw and the car park. After reaching the ridge at 607 548, it would be better to go down the path which follows the railway to the town of Llanberis.

2.4 Route cards

All the route planning information discussed so far should be written down on a **route card**. The route should be broken down into stages, as we did in Exercise 9 when choosing the route.

For each stage work out and write down:
1. the distance
2. the height gained (If there are no spot heights, count the uphill contours which are 10 metres apart and the thicker contours which are 50 metres apart.)
3. the time
4. the compass bearing to the next stage
5. the grid reference.

OBJECTIVE:					Date:
Location	Grid Reference	Magnetic Bearing	Distance	Height	Time

Time for Rests:
Time out =   Expected Time Back:
ESCAPE ROUTES
① ② ③

It is important that everyone in the group knows the planned route and has drawn it in pencil on his or her map. This adds to the enjoyment of the walk as well as the safety of it. Finally, before setting out, *always check the weather forecast* and prepare for the worst (more about weather hazards in Chapter 3).

> *Exercise 12*
> Divide the Snowdon route into about four stages. For each one write down the five pieces of information as shown in the diagram below.

OBJECTIVE = Snowdon					Date:
Location	Grid Reference	Magnetic Bearing	Distance	Height	Time
YHA	647557				
Ridge	635553	252°	1.5 km	25 m	25 min

3 MOUNTAIN SAFETY

All mountaineering involves some risk, and to some people, this is part of the attraction of mountains. Even though you may be properly equipped and have planned the route carefully, the potential dangers and hazards mean that you should always be prepared for the worst. In this Section, we shall look at the hazards and how to try to avoid accidents; and also how to reduce the dangers if an accident does happen.

3.1 Mountain accidents

Every accident in the mountains is serious by the very nature of the environment. The main problems with the mountain environment are its remoteness from sources of help, the weather (which can change quickly), the difficulty of the terrain and the delay between accident time and medical treatment. This delay can occasionally be fatal, and it is therefore up to every mountaineer to know how to reduce it.

MOUNTAIN WALKING

Over the years, the number of accidents in the mountains of Britain has been increasing. This is partly because of the growing popularity of the hills and mountains for recreation. We have already mentioned some of the main reasons why accidents occur:
1. lack of the right equipment and clothing
2. getting lost due to poor navigation.

Other reasons include:

3. slips on rock
4. underestimating the weather
5. not knowing what to do or how to cope.

The following table shows the number of reported accidents in the two years 1967 and 1977 for walking and climbing activities in Britain. The figures in brackets show how many of these accidents proved fatal.

	Reported accidents	
	1967	1977
Walking	115 (17)	160 (16)
Climbing	63 (10)	95 (18)
Total	183 (27)	255 (34)

Accident reports from Wales, Pennines, Scotland and the Lake District, from the Mountain Rescue Committee's accident report records.

From the table, you can see that the total number of reported accidents in the ten years from 1967 to 1977 increased by around 40%. A similar picture is expected for the ten years to 1987. From these figures it would seem that walking is more dangerous than climbing, but we must not forget that more people go walking than climbing, so more walking accidents are likely to occur anyway.

Two-fifths of all the accidents happened to people under twenty-one. This may be due to the large number of school, college, scouts and adventure holiday trips, which often include people who have no real experience or knowledge of the mountains.

The kinds of minor accidents that will always happen, no matter how careful you are, include: cuts, grazes, sprains, and so on. To deal with these, you should carry, or have access to, a first-aid kit which should include the following items:

1. triangular bandage
2. sterile dressing
3. lint dressing
4. other bandages
5. plasters
6. antiseptic cream
7. safety pins
8. paracetamol tablets

What to do in the event of more serious accidents is covered in Appendix A.

Mountain rescue teams cover all Britain's mountain areas. These teams are made up of experienced local mountaineers who join together to turn out at any time to give help, such as searching for lost people or carrying injured walkers and climbers off the mountain. Except in cases of minor injury, they should be called for immediately.

Mountain rescue teams may use dogs to search for lost climbers

MOUNTAIN SAFETY

Mountain rescue posts are identified by a sign outside the building and they are marked on OS maps. At each post, there is rescue equipment. This consists of a stretcher, rucksacks containing medical supplies, sleeping bags, warm clothing and sometimes cooking gear. The supervisors at these posts set the rescues into operation and usually organise and lead rescue parties.

Exercise 13
Find the mountain rescue posts at 648 603 and 650 603. Now locate the nearest two posts to our Snowdon route.

3.2 Sending for help

If a casualty cannot be moved, then help is needed from the rescue services. First of all make sure the casualty is safe, comfortable and sheltered from the wind and rain. You will then need to put together an **emergency bivouac**. A bivouac is a temporary shelter made from whatever items you have, such as rucksacks, polythene bag, even a tent's flysheet. Follow this procedure:

1. Choose a place which is sheltered from the wind, such as behind a stone wall.
2. Put extra dry clothing on the casualty and put them into a sleeping bag.
3. Make a bivouac. The best way is to use a special, large bag (called a **survival** or **bivy bag**) which has holes in it to help with breathing. Bivy bags are usually bright orange in colour to make them easy to spot by the rescuers. Put the casualty into a rucksack, and sit them on rope or anything else which will insulate them from the cold ground. Finally, put the survival bag over them.

When the casualty and the rest of the group are safe, a messenger will need to go and get help, taking the easiest escape route down and carrying a note explaining:
1. the grid reference of the accident plus a description of the location e.g. GR 632 548, 100 m W of causeway on Miner's Track
2. accident details
3. numbers involved in the accident.

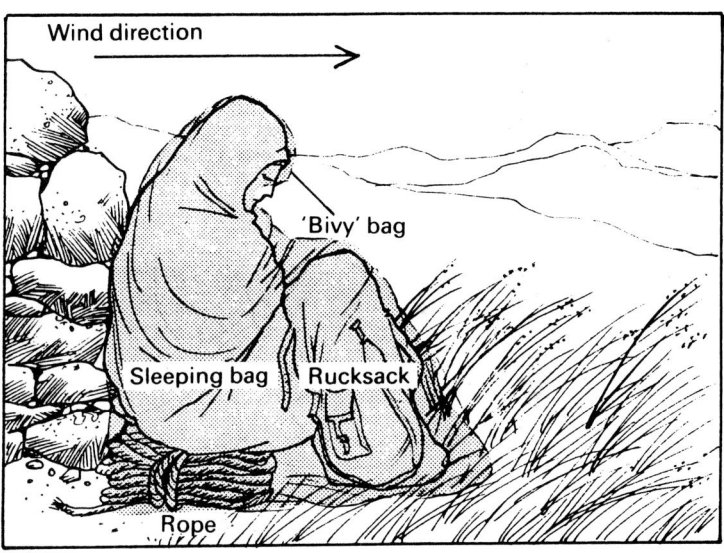

An emergency bivouac

MOUNTAIN WALKING

If you are not too sure of the grid reference, take a compass bearing from where you are to two or three surrounding features, such as mountain summits. From these, the rescue teams will be able to work out where you are.

> *Exercise 14*
> Construct bivouacs using whatever materials you have at hand.

3.3 Getting down after an accident

If you can get the casualty down without calling out the Mountain Rescue, then do so, but make sure this can be done safely and relatively easily. If the casualty can walk, carry their equipment for them. If they cannot walk, and if the distance involved is not too far, there are ways of carrying them down, but these are uncomfortable and exhausting for everyone. Three such methods are described below.

1 Rucksack carry
All you need for this is an empty rucksack in which the casualty sits with their legs fully through the extended straps.

2 Split-rope carry
For this, you need a coiled rope which is separated into two. Extra padding can be added to make it more comfortable for the casualty.

3 Rope stretcher
For this, all you need is a rope and a sleeping bag. Lay the rope down in a series of loops. Put the casualty into the sleeping bag and onto the loops. Then tie an overhand knot at the foot end and thread the next loop through it. Continue lacing the loops up to the chest and tie off. Take the free end under the head of the casualty for support, and tie two overhand knots, then take the rope down the body towards the toes putting in overhand knots at intervals for six people to carry.

Rucksack carry

Split-rope carry

MOUNTAIN SAFETY

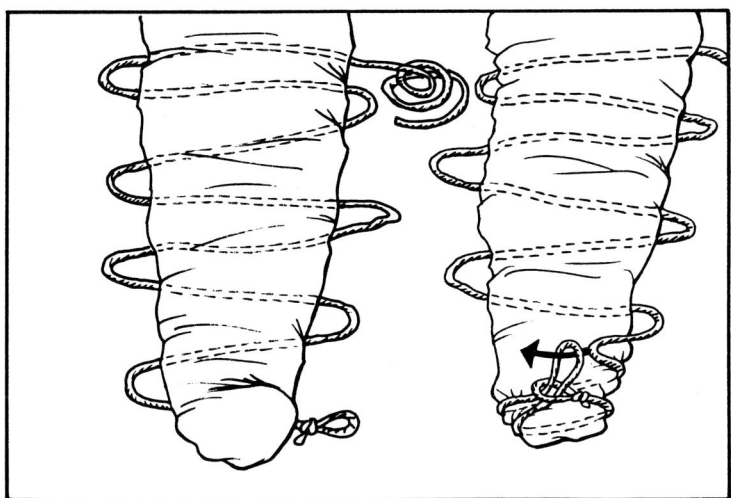

How to start making a rope stretcher using a sleeping bag

Exposure to any of these factors may cause hypothermia

> *Exercise 15*
> Try out the three carrying methods on friends. Find out which you prefer when you are carrying, and also when you are the person being carried.

3.4 Mountain hypothermia

For years the term hypothermia has been used to describe a very real and threatening problem for mountaineers. The effect of such things as cold and exhaustion on the body can cause our temperature to drop. When our body temperature gets too low, we can't keep functioning and eventually, if help isn't given, someone suffering from exposure will die. 'Exposure' to bad weather, although important, is however only one of the causes. As the diagram above shows, it is usually a combination of things which causes a drop in body heat, and so it is more accurate to call this condition **mountain hypothermia**.

Basically, the problem is not so much to do with getting cold, but more to do with the effect of this on the **inner core** temperature of the body (the parts of the body that are deep inside the chest, abdomen and head, where our essential life-maintaining organs are located). The inner core temperature is around 37°C. If this was to drop to about 31°C your brain and the coordination of your muscles would be affected. If it dropped a little more, you would become unconscious, and at about 28°C your heart, lungs and brain would cease functioning and you would die.

DANGEROUS   *SIGNS OF HYPOTHERMIA*   *LIFE-THREATENING EMERGENCY*

Shivering,
Stumbling,
'Not caring'...  *Slow thinking,*
strange behaviour,
body stiff....  *Unconscious....*

MOUNTAIN WALKING

The problem is that once your inner core begins to cool, virtually nothing can be done to warm it up again. The old treatments of rubbing hands and drinking alcohol from a St. Bernard dog only speed up death because both encourage increased blood movement from the warmer core to the cooler surface, so further accelerating the heat loss from the core and replacing warm blood inside the body with cold blood from the surface.

A person can show a number of signs which indicate that they are suffering from, or moving towards, mountain hypothermia. What can you do if you notice a person moving towards this condition? In simple terms, the immediate things to do are:

1. Stop.
2. Find shelter out of the wind as quickly as possible.
3. Take wet clothes off the victim and replace with dry spare clothing. (But if the victim is clearly already suffering from mountain hypothermia, do *not* remove wet clothing.)
4. Put the victim in a sleeping bag (if available) and inside a survival 'bivy' bag. Insulate the victim from the cold ground with rucksack, etc.
5. Feed—give the victim a hot drink and food such as chocolate or biscuits.

If the casualty does not respond by this time, then extra heat must be added. This can be provided by a fit member of the group getting into the sleeping bag with the victim.

If the casualty still does not respond, or is unconscious, then keep the person insulated and go for help. Keep the casualty's head low to aid circulation of the blood between brain, heart and lungs.

If the casualty was in the early stages of hypothermia and recovers quickly (unlikely to take less than half an hour), then he or she could be allowed to walk off the mountain. Always remember that it is far better to avoid cases of hypothermia than to treat them. In cold, wet and windy conditions, or if a walk is proving too exhausting, it is best not to continue but to turn back or find an escape route down the mountain.

3.5 Getting lost

If you keep checking your map and have planned your route properly, then you should always know where you are. But if you ever do get lost, it's often difficult to decide whether to keep going, in the hope that you will eventually get back on route, or to stop. This decision may depend on the weather and the time of day. If the weather is bad, or if it's getting towards night time, it is best to stop and bivouac until the morning or until things improve, particularly in the case of mountain mist, which can come down suddenly at any time of day. Wandering around, lost in mist, is *extremely dangerous*.

You should find shelter, put on extra clothing, sit in rucksacks and construct whatever bivouac you can to keep warm. If you had left a note of the route with someone at the start of the walk, rescue teams may already be looking for you. A mountain rescue signal which you can use in an emergency to attract attention is

The rescue team consists of local volunteer mountaineers with a good knowledge of the area

the **International Alpine Distress Signal**. You can send this signal using a torch, a whistle or your voice. It consists of six quick flashes, blasts or calls with a one minute interval before you repeat. In reply, you would see three quick flashes, blasts or calls, repeated after one minute.

If you see or hear the distress signal when you are in the mountains, it's important to take a compass bearing of the direction it's coming from and note it down. Give the reply and move towards it or report to the rescue teams. It is traditional that if someone is in trouble, mountaineers will give help wherever possible and assist the recue teams if required.

Exercise 16
To practise your leadership qualities in emergency situations, go for a local walk and take sealed envelopes in which you have written details of emergency situations, such as, 'It is nearly night, you are lost—what should you do?' Take it in turns to set the pace and become leader. After a while, choose an envelope, read the emergency situation and do what you think is best.

Conclusion

In this Chapter, you have learned something about walking in the mountains and what to do if things go wrong. Once you have experienced the mountains yourself, you will be able to go on longer routes and plan for expeditions (Chapter 3).

? FURTHER INFORMATION

Organisations

The governing body for mountain activities in Britain is the British Mountaineering Council, Crawford House, Precinct Centre, Booth Street East, Manchester M13 9RZ. Enquiries about membership, etc. should be directed to the General Secretary. Members of the British Mountaineering Council (BMC) receive a monthly magazine called High.

For those particularly interested in Scotland, The Mountaineering Council of Scotland can be contacted at 15 Dowies Mill Lane, Cramond, Edinburgh EH4 6DW.

Magazines

The Great Outdoors from newsagents or the publisher: Holmes McDougall Ltd, Ravenseft House, 302 St Vincent Street, Glasgow G2 5NL

Climber (as above)

Books

Mountaincraft and Leadership by E. Langmuir is available from the British Mountaineering Council.

Mountaineering by A. Blackshaw was published by Penguin in 1970 but still contains much useful information.

Suitable guidebooks to the main mountain areas in Britain are published by Constable and Co. Ltd, 10 Orange Street, London WC2H 7EG

Courses

Courses are organised by Centres in Wales and Scotland. Write for details to:
The National Centre for Mountain Activities, Plas-Y-Brenin, Capel Curig, Betws-Y-Coed, Gwynedd, North Wales LL24 0ET.

National Outdoor Training Centre, Glenmore Lodge, Aviemore, Inverness-shire, Scotland PH22 1QU.

The BMC coordinates courses, such as the Mountain Leader's Certificate. Write for details.

Mountain Rescue Committee

This organisation produces a yearly handbook which lists rescue teams and posts as well as details of safety and statistics. The handbook can be obtained from:
The Secretary, Mountain Rescue Committee, 9 Milldale Avenue, Temple Meads, Buxton, Derbyshire SK17 9BE.

WORKSHEET

1. What are the highest mountains in Scotland, Wales and England?

2. Why do you think many accidents happen when walking down a mountain?

3. Why shouldn't you be tempted to avoid picking escape routes until you need them?

4. Draw a diagram showing the signs of mountain hypothermia.

5. It is not a good idea to drink alcohol or rub the skin when cold. Why?

6. What is the International Alpine Distress Signal and the reply?

7. Why are heavy leather boots sometimes called 'a pair of leather coffins'?

8. List three things that you should think about when choosing a resting place.

9. You ought to carry or have access to a basic first-aid kit. List the items it should contain.

To answer questions 10, 11 and 12 you will need to read Appendix A—First Aid.

10. To test if a person is unconscious, you could . . . (complete in a few sentences)

11. In first aid, what does ABC mean?

12. It is important to raise a bleeding limb, because . . . (complete)

13. Explain the effect of hypothermia on the body.

14. What is the job of (a) inner clothes? (b) outer clothes?

15. Why is it not a good idea to wear a 'cag' all the time?

16. In treating mountain hypothermia, explain why you should STOP, INSULATE and FEED the victim.

17. Describe what you would do in this situation: you are the leader, high in the mountains, when one of your group falls and looks unconscious.

The next three questions are to be answered together to form a short essay. Question 18 is the introduction, question 19 is the main part of the essay and question 20, the conclusion.

Title: **Accidents in the British Mountains**

18. What are the particular dangers of the mountains?

19. Why have the numbers of mountain accidents been increasing? Describe the mountain rescue service, and how and when to use it.

20. Are accidents avoidable? If so, what should be done to prevent them?

© Ian Lockren 1988   Permission is given to photocopy the above worksheet without fee for use in the institution by which the book is bought.

3 CAMPING AND EXPEDITIONS

Equipment List

Catalogues—tents
  —rucksacks
  —sleeping bags
  —stoves

Lightweight tent

Safety rope

Stove, fuel, matches

Packet-soup

Weather chart from newspaper

Mountain map (Snowdon)

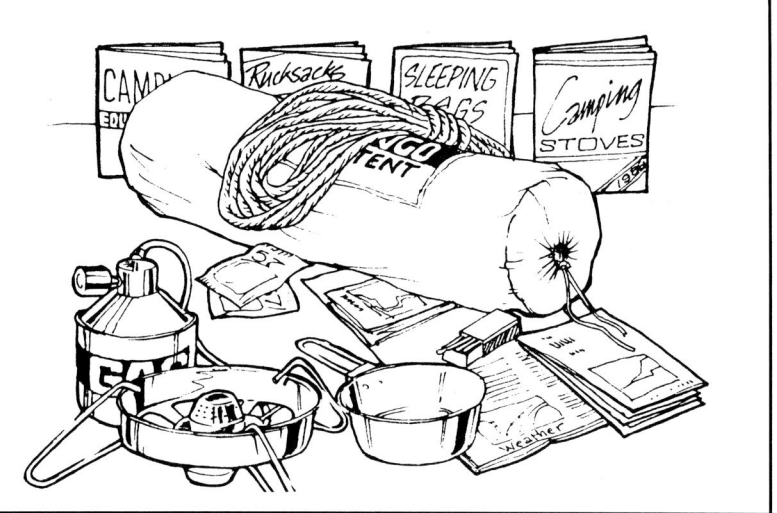

Introduction

Camping in the mountain areas of Britain has become very popular for a variety of reasons. Some people prefer to camp in the valleys, making this the **base camp** for their equipment and overnight stays, and taking with them only what is needed for their day's walk or climb. Others carry their equipment, food and clothes with them all the time in their rucksacks. This is called **backpacking** and is regarded as taking mountain walking a stage further so that you have more of a feeling of adventure, by camping in a different place each night.

Many mountaineers prefer backpacking because of the freedom it gives; it also saves the money you would spend on camp site fees. This Chapter is mainly about backpacking but the camping skills and information will prepare you for expeditions of one night or several, and can be applied to any sort of camping.

1 LIGHTWEIGHT CAMPING EQUIPMENT

If you travel to a camp site by car or minibus and use this as a base camp then within reason, there is little restriction on the amount of equipment you take with you. When backpacking, however, because you have got to carry all your equipment on your back, exactly how much you take becomes much more important. A balance must be found between only taking the bare essentials such as a tent and food, and having with you those things that make life rather more comfortable. The golden rule in this respect is that your total load should not be more than one third of your body weight, or an absolute maximum of 14 kg for younger people. Not so long ago, trying to keep a light load was a real problem, but the recent development of lightweight synthetic materials and food has revolutionised life for the backpacker.

1.1 Lightweight tents

The weight of a tent is important, but so, too, is the living space it gives and its performance in the rain. When choosing a tent, a backpacker will consider all of these and decide which is the more important. For example, a heavier tent would be more stable and have plenty of room inside, whereas one that is lighter will be smaller and less resistant to strong mountain winds. Even so, every mountain tent should have these qualities:

1 It should be strong.
2 It should be easy to put up.
3 It should have two 'skins' (an inner tent and an outer fly sheet).

An **inner tent** should always have a strong, waterproof, sewn-in ground sheet which extends a little way up the sides. A **fly sheet** is basically an extra roof which gives added protection from the weather. As well as covering the inner tent, the flysheet should also extend at the front to give extra room to store equipment and cook. Keeping a space between the two skins is important. It provides insulation, keeping the inside of the tent warmer in cold weather and cooler in hot weather. If the two skins come into contact, the inner tent might leak.

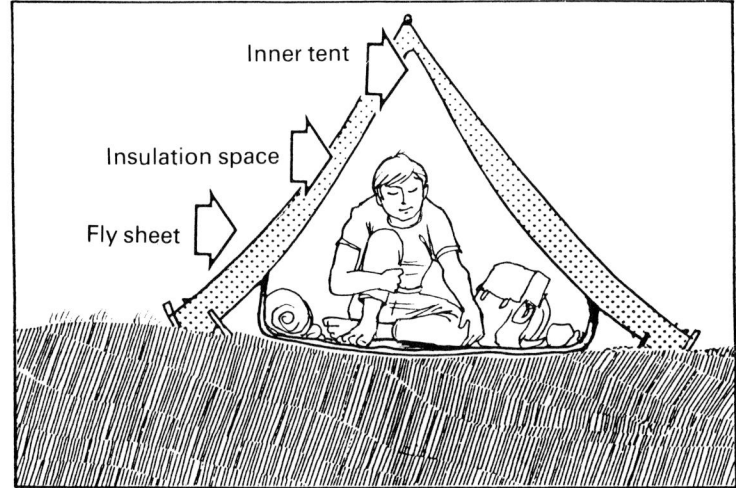

The two 'skins' of a tent should be kept apart

These are not the only reasons why a flysheet is essential. A single-skin tent made from cotton or canvas, which 'breathes', helps to cut down the condensation which would otherwise collect on the insides of the tent during the night, wetting clothes and equipment. Yet it has the distinct disadvantage that when it rains, the threads of natural fibre swell and absorb up to half their own weight of water. This makes such a tent heavy and it takes a long time to dry out.

A waterproofed nylon tent is very light and has the advantage that, in wet weather, the backpacker is able to shake off ninety per-cent of the rainwater on its surface, before packing the tent and carrying it. However, with this material, comes the problem of condensation. Who wants to wake up in a nylon bath?

A cotton tent gets heavy when wet

Therefore the best solution is to have a proofed nylon flysheet which keeps out the rain (instead of absorbing it), an inner tent with sides that can 'breathe' (made from cotton or lightweight nylon) and a proofed ground sheet.

CAMPING AND EXPEDITIONS

A two-skin ridge tent

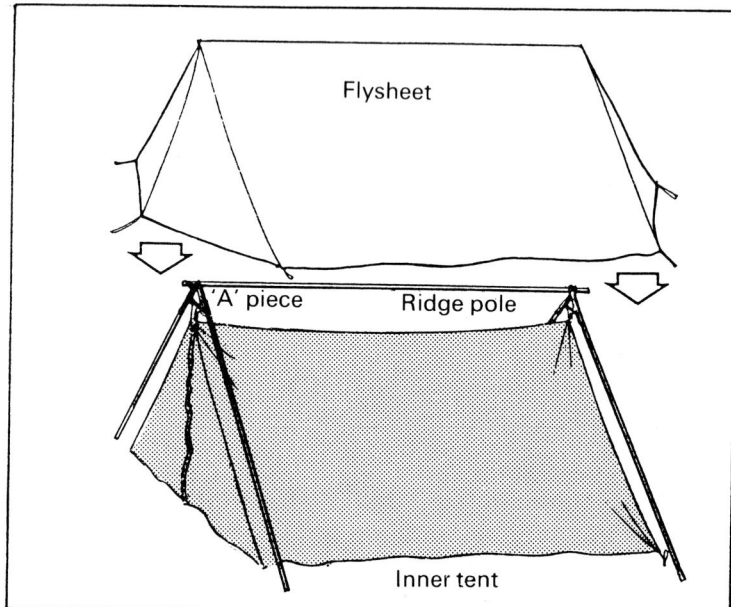

The flysheet is draped over the inner tent

There are a vast number of different shapes and sizes of lightweight tent to choose from. They range from **(1)** the traditional triangular-shaped ridge tent to **(2)** the modern, sometimes weirdly-shaped hooped and dome tents with flexible poles.

(1) A traditional lightweight tent, such as one of the Vango series, has a ridge pole supported at each end by external poles. The cotton inner tent is hooked on and hangs from the 'A' pieces at the front and back, and the flysheet is draped over the frame of ridge and poles (see the diagram on top right). The two skins are kept taut by the pull of side guys and rubber shock-cord guys. This looks and is, a solid type of tent which, although weighing at least 4 kg, is ideal for high-level and bad weather camping.

Attempts have been made to reduce the weight of the ridge tent for the backpacker by sacrificing some of the strength and ease of access. The diagram opposite shows the frames of lighter tents, both with ridges which slope down to a shorter single internal rear pole. The lighter model reduces the weight even more by doing away with the front external poles. This makes getting into and out of the tent more difficult, and it also cuts down on the space available inside. Some backpackers prefer to carry the extra weight of a slightly larger or roomier tent.

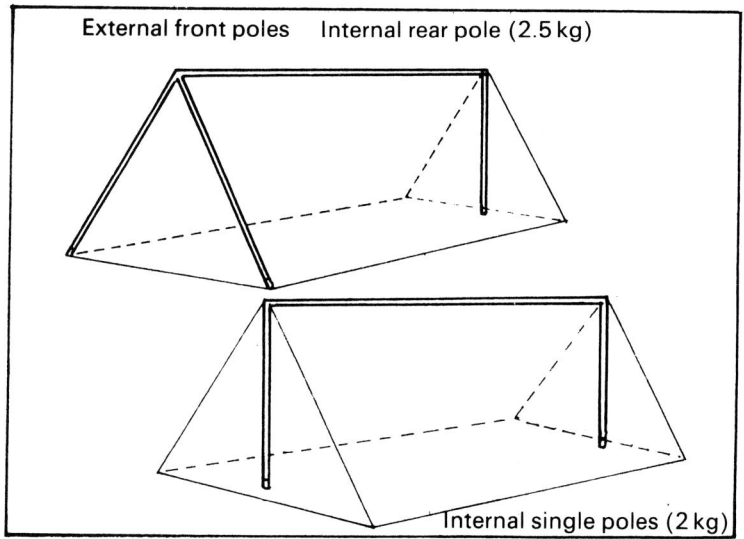

Light ridge tents, with fewer poles

CAMPING EQUIPMENT

(2) Modern flexible-pole tents attempt to resolve the problem of 'the lighter the tent, the smaller the living space'. In other words they try to marry maximum space with minimum weight, and in many cases they succeed in doing so. How do they do it? Basically its done by using synthetic, lightweight, flexible poles which not only support, but also push and hold out the tent. The result is hoops and domes of various forms and shapes. These tents provide more space than ridge tents of the same height and weight.

The early types of flexible-pole tents were very wobbly—like jelly in the wind. Recent designs have, to a large extent, reduced this by the use of guy systems. The most stable tents have three flexible poles, or hoops, crossing each other and weighing around 4.5 kg. Two-pole cross-over or single-pole hoops are lighter (some weigh below 2 kg) but they are generally not as strong.

Ridge tents will always be popular, particularly in high level camping, because of their safe and solid characteristics, but flexible hoops and domes do offer more space for weight and are definitely here to stay.

Points to remember:
1. Always use a two-skin tent.
2. The flysheet should be made of proofed nylon and the sides of the inner tent should be made of breathable material. There should be a coated ground sheet.
3. For more space and low weight, hoops or domes should be chosen.
4. For security, a ridge tent should be chosen.
5. If buying, choose the best you can afford.

Exercise 1
1. From a collection of tent catalogues, select the best examples of lightweight tent for each category: one man; two man; larger tent. Look for weight, type, any additional features and price.
2. Discuss your selections with the rest of the group.

A 'hooped' tent uses flexible poles

1.2 Sleeping bags

A **sleeping bag** is a very important piece of mountain camping equipment. Its main job is to keep you warm and comfortable by insulating your body from the cold air and ground. The amount of insulation depends not only on **(1)** what the bag is filled with, but also **(2)** how this filling is arranged within the bag.

(1) Bags should contain either natural filling, such as **down** and **feathers**, or man-made material such as **terylene** or **hollowfill**. Down, which is the small, fluffy underfeathers of geese and ducks, is the best filling. It is light, very warm, soft and difficult to compress. The addition of larger feathers to the down mixture helps to reduce the cost without losing too much in warmth. However a down bag becomes useless if allowed to get wet! Recently, synthetic fillings have been produced which dry out more quickly and are cheaper. Bags with synthetic fillings can be used in mountain conditions but, weight for weight, in very cold conditions, down is better.

(2) The filling needs to be fixed in place inside the bag so that it does not bunch together and create gaps which would allow body heat to escape. (Such gaps are called **cold spots**.) The following diagram shows three different ways of holding a sleeping bag's filling in place. Where the inside and outside walls of the bag are stitched together, as in (a), cold spots are formed. In (b) and (c), the two walls are kept apart so that there are no cold spots. Whatever the filling or its arrangement between the walls, a bag can only provide warmth by holding in body heat. For this reason, most mountain-type bags have draw-cords or head covers to trap heat, and they do not have zips, which allow heat to escape.

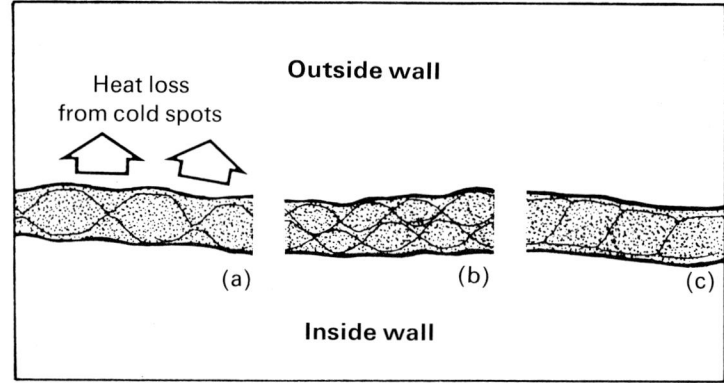

Cross-section of three types of sleeping bag

Exercise 2

In most homes you will find at least one sleeping bag. If you have access to one, find out:
1. What filling it has.
2. How the filling is stitched in place.
3. Whether or not it would be of value in the mountains.

(*Note: if you have two cheap, thin, zipped bags, you can always put one inside the other. Remember, however, not to have both zips on the same side.*)

A suitable sleeping bag

1.3 Stoves

Hot food is essential for anyone planning to spend even one night out of doors in the mountains. There are three ways of heating up food.

1. You could work on an open fire. This however is not advisable. Quite apart from the problem of a lack of wood in the mountains, and the time and trouble it takes to get a fire going, there is the harm it does to the ground—unsightly fire rings will spoil the area for others.
2. You can buy 'hot cans'. These are self-heating tins which warm up the food inside. However they are relatively expensive and heavy to carry.
3. If you are not planning to use either of these methods (and most backpackers don't) you will need to carry and use a stove (the most usual method). There are a variety of lightweight stoves available. Some burn solid fuel and petrol, but most useful are those using (a) gas, (b) paraffin or (c) methylated spirits (meths).

CAMPING EQUIPMENT

(a) Gas stoves

Cooking with gas is the most popular and probably the easiest method to use. The gas comes in sealed cartridges and once lit, the flame is usually very easy to adjust. Gas stoves are also often lighter and cheaper, even though the cartridges are usually more costly to replace than equivalent refills for paraffin or meths stoves. The gas inside the cartridges varies between manufacturers. The best combination, which burns in all weathers, is a butane/propane mix. Camping Gaz stoves are probably the most popular. Recent developments include models which come complete with their own very light pots. These are likely to become popular in the future.

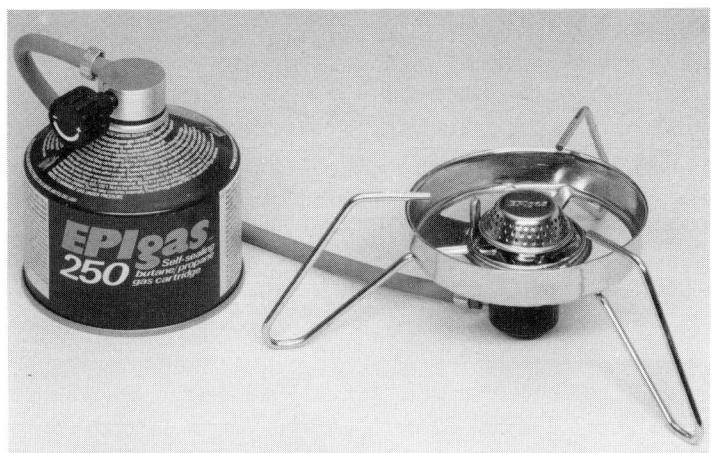

Modern gas stoves are light and convenient

(b) Paraffin stoves

A stove fuelled by paraffin can be difficult to light. The burner requires pre-heating with meths before closing the air valve and pumping paraffin under pressure to the burner. One of three things could then happen:

1. Nothing! This means you waited too long. The meths has gone out and you need to re-light the burner with a match and repeat the pumping.
2. A 'flare-up'. You pumped too soon and flooded the burner with meths and paraffin. Release the air valve to cut off the supply of paraffin and wait for the stove to 'calm down', then try again.
3. The paraffin ignites and roars into action, ready for use. Success! After this, if the heat needs increasing, simply add more pressure by pumping; or if the flame needs lowering, open the air valve a little to release some of the pressure.

After use, open the air valve. The paraffin will stop going to the burner and the flame should go out. As you can see, using a stove of this type requires some practice, plenty of patience and more than a little courage! The most well known paraffin stove is the **Primus** which is cheap to run, has a high heat output and can burn for a long time.

Paraffin stoves are more difficult to use

CAMPING AND EXPEDITIONS

(c) Meths stoves

This sort of stove was used widely before gas cartridges became available. It is simple and cheap, but is perhaps not as convenient or as clean as other types. However, unlike the other fuels, the meths is burnt unpressurised and so for this reason, it is probably the safest to use. The meths is usually burnt in an open cup protected by a windshield. Some makes, such as the world famous **Trangia** come complete with a set of lightweight pans.

Meths stoves are simple and cheap

> *Exercise 3*
> Practise lighting, putting out and cooking on a lightweight stove. Try simple things first such as packet soups, tea or coffee.

1.4 Rucksacks

The rucksack has proved to be the only tried-and-tested way of carrying heavy loads over any real distance. Since you will need a sack which can hold all your requirements for your stay in the mountains, it will have to be larger, stronger and have more built-in comfort than the types of daysack discussed in Chapter 2 (Section 1.6). It is best to have a sack that is long rather than wide, and it should also allow most of the equipment to be high up, rather than low down in position within the sack. The reason for this is that it is less tiring to have weight on your shoulders than further down on your back.

A backpacking rucksack should be larger than a day sack, with more pockets and more emphasis on comfort

CAMPING EQUIPMENT

Designers of rucksacks have tried to reduce the strain on the back still further by using broad waist and shoulder straps. Sacks with a strong external frame also help to spread the load. However such frames do, in fact, hold all the weight *away* from the back, and the result is a feeling of instability when walking. Therefore, more recent designs have placed flat aluminium frames (shaped to fit into the natural curve of the back) inside the sack. One disadvantage of a sack that hugs the body so closely is that, because the air cannot circulate and evaporate sweat, wetness tends to build up on skin and clothes. This eventually chills the back and can lead to muscle strain and pain. So to counteract this as much as possible, ventilation channels are built into the padding. Another recent development is the hip belt (as opposed to the waist belt) which transfers a portion of the load on to the hips.

However, undoubtedly the best contribution to bring ease and comfort has been the invention of the **adjustable rucksack**. No matter how tall or small you are, this type of sack can adjust to fit the size of your back. Gone are the days of the sack which did not feel quite right and became increasingly uncomfortable as time wore on.

Points to remember:

Ideally, for a sack to fit with ease and comfort, it should have:
1 broad shoulder straps, which adjust for width and length
2 comfortable hip belt
3 shaped internal frame
4 ventilation channels

Exercise 4
Check out the types of rucksack available by picking out the best examples from catalogues. Add to the list of qualities the things that are important to you. Then design, draw and label your ideal rucksack.

Exercise 5
Check out the tents, bags, stoves and rucksacks owned by your school/college/club/group. Evaluate the choice available to you. For example, decide which you like or dislike, which you find easy or difficult to use. Could any of the equipment be usefully updated?

External frame rucksacks can be awkward

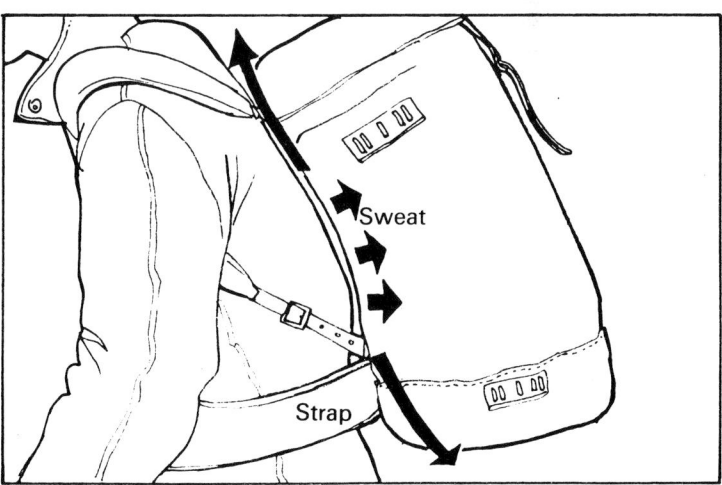

Good air circulation helps evaporate sweat

CAMPING AND EXPEDITIONS

2 HOW TO CAMP

In this Section we shall look at using the camping equipment discussed in Section 1, so that our mountain camp is as safe and comfortable as possible. All the advice that appeared in the previous Chapter on Mountain Walking should be followed. The only differences are, first, the load being carried is greater on a camping trip, so the pace should be slower. Secondly, the route planning stage must take into account the extra number of days and nights that will be spent in the mountains.

2.1 Loading up

Additions to your normal load should include items designed to provide safety and give comfort, such as extra clothes to be used only at night or in an emergency, toilet and washing requirements, food, fuel, a water carrier and cooking and cleaning utensils. It is a good idea to line your rucksack with a polythene bag, or at least protect the items you do not want to get wet, such as sleeping bag and clothes. Each tent and its occupants should be self-sufficient in food, fuel and safety equipment.

A number of shared items can be divided between the individual members of each tent. For example, in a group of three, one carries the poles and pegs, another the flysheet and the third the inner tent. This also applies to other shared articles of equipment and food. It is an art to be able to pack a sack so that everything is in the best possible place to give balance, stability and comfort. You can normally guarantee something will be sticking into your back, or there is an irritating rattle when you walk, or your toothpaste squeezes out onto the week's supply of bread! However, if you follow the suggested packing arrangement below you will have a better chance of avoiding pitfalls.

Points to remember:
1. Pack heavy items towards the top.
2. Pack things needed during the journey, or immediately on reaching the campsite, on the top or in side pockets.
3. Pack stove and fuel separate from other things— either in a strong polythene bag or in a side pocket.
4. Your total load should not be more than one third of your body weight, or 14 kg for younger backpackers.

Finally, if your rucksack is too heavy or bulky all that you will get from your trek will be pain and misery—don't turn *backpacking* into a *backbreaking* experience!

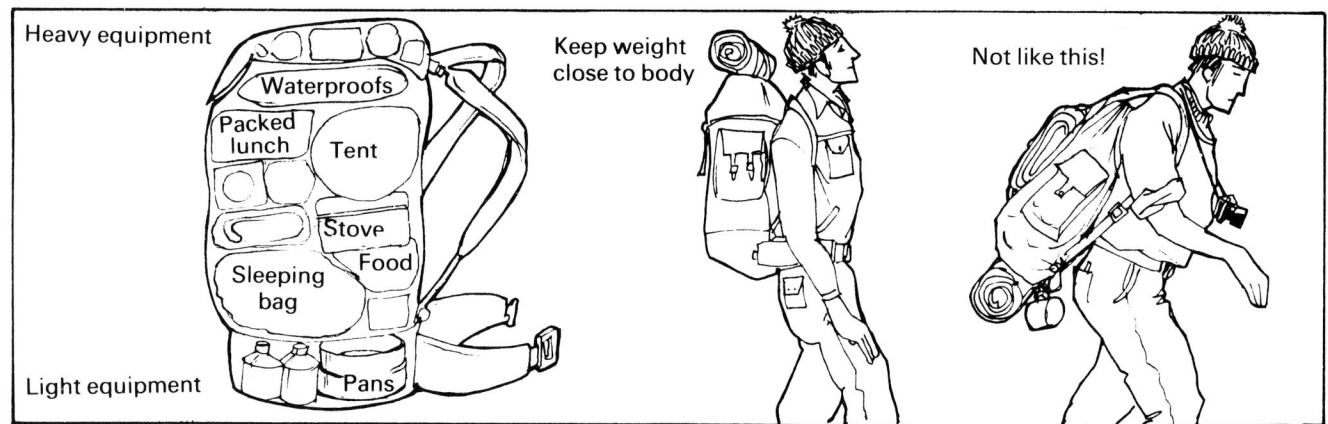

Aim for comfort and convenience when packing a rucksack

> *Exercise 6—A whole group activity*
> 1 Decide on an agreed checklist of equipment and personal effects necessary for one person to have in a rucksack for a one night camp.
> 2 As far as possible, put together this checklist of items from equipment at hand, and from each person bringing in some article of spare clothing or food, etc. If you can, weigh the finished sack.
> 3 Divide the group into teams for a pack-loading competition.

2.2 Making camp—choosing the site

It is best to have the camp site or target area selected beforehand, as part of normal route planning. Aim to reach it at least two hours before dark. This will give plenty of time to set-up camp and eat in the daylight. The following diagram shows a number of considerations to bear in mind when choosing the site. The main ones are that the site should be:
1 sheltered from wind, but not directly under trees.
2 a dryish area, not marshy or likely to flood—short springy grass is often a sign of dry ground.
3 on flat ground. Avoid sleeping on slopes, but if you have no choice, lie with your head up-slope.
4 close to water for cooking, washing and for keeping food which might go off, cool.
5 Remember that even land high in the mountains belongs to someone. Find out if you need permission to camp beforehand; even if you don't, look after the site and the surrounding environment.

> *Exercise 7*
> For this exercise, you require your mountain map (Snowdon, sheet 115). The expedition is an overnight camp-walking trip from the road at 687 603. The first day is to take in Ffynnon Llugwy Reservoir and the summit of Carnedd Llewelyn (684 644). An overnight camp will be followed by a walk on the second day to reach the car park at 663 719 by mid-afternoon.
> What you will have to do...
> 1 Select a route from the start to the finish of the trip.
> 2 Select a camp site somewhere along this route, trying not to leave yourself too much walking on the second day.
>
> **Weather Conditions:** A light wind coming from the west, picking up to strong overnight.

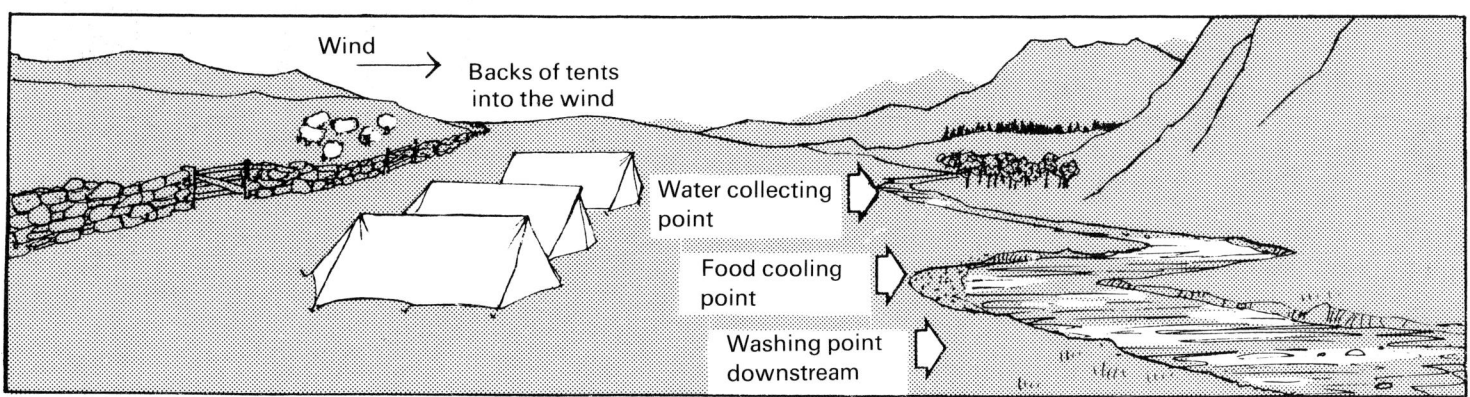

Choose your site carefully

2.3 Making camp—pitching tents

On reaching the site of a camp, the first thing to do is to put up the tents. You will notice from the diagram on page 53 that the tents are sited on the higher ground, with the back ends pointing into the wind. However, if the weather forecast is good, you may prefer to have the front opening up to the morning sun (i.e. facing south-east).

It is important that every member of a party is familiar with tent equipment, to be able to put up (*pitch*), take down (*strike*) and pack away with speed. Any delay, in, for example, pitching a tent in hostile weather, could increase the chance of someone suffering from mountain hypothermia.

The following guidelines are based on pitching a tent of the Vango Force Ten type, but could be applied to most types of lightweight ridge tent.

1. Note how the tent fits into its bag and how it was folded.
2. Spread the inner tent on the ground, making sure the front door is zipped up.
3. Insert the pegs into the ground sheet guys, starting at one of the back corners and then working to the other corners. Keep the ground sheet fully extended when inserting the pegs.
4. Fit the poles together (including the 'A' pieces) and insert the rear spindle into the ridge.
5. Place the rear poles in line with the seams of the tent, and suspend the tent from the back 'A' piece.
6. Repeat 5 at the front end of the tent.
7. Insert the pegs into the wall guys—corners first.
8. Adjust the pull of the guys as necessary so that the tent is not puckered (the side guys should normally be in line with the seams, following the same slope as the roof).
9. Drape the zipped-up flysheet over and peg it down evenly, making sure it is not touching the inner tent at any point.

To pack the tent away, reverse the above sequence, but if the flysheet is wet, allow it to dry beforehand if you can. (If not, make sure you unpack it later so that it gets the chance to dry thoroughly. If you don't do this the nylon, zips, etc. will end up covered in mildew). Make sure you also clean both the pegs and the underside of the tent before packing.

Exercise 8

Divide the group into teams and hold tent putting-up, taking-down and packing-away competitions against the clock. Add penalty points for faults like puckered sides, pegs in the wrong position or in-effective pegs.

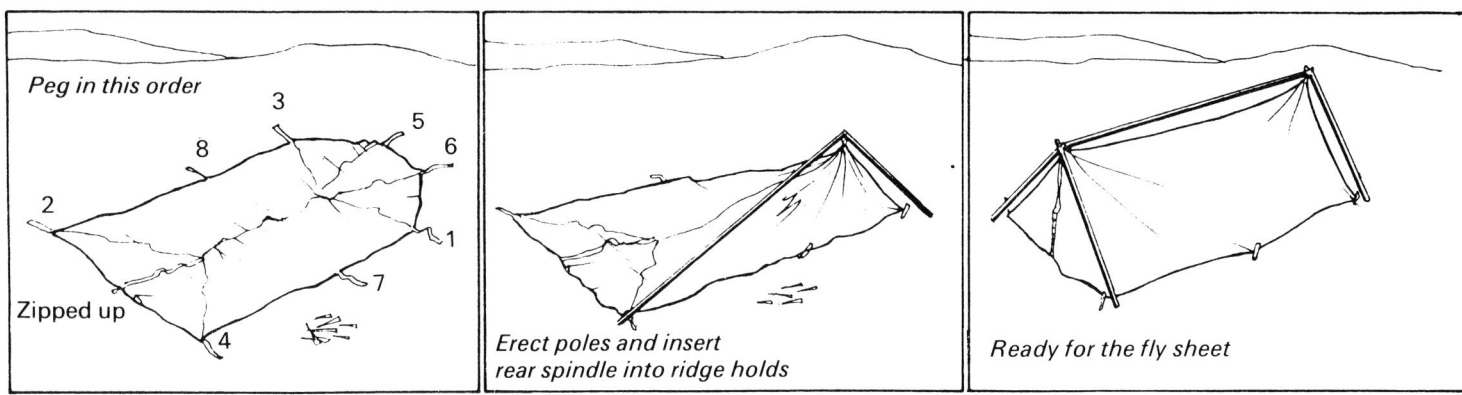

Peg in this order / Zipped up

Erect poles and insert rear spindle into ridge holds

Ready for the fly sheet

> *Exercise 9*
> If the weather forecast is not good, there are several things you can do to strengthen the tent and pegs in preparation for storms:
> 1 Attach additional storm guys from each pole spindle.
> 2 Double-peg the guys or place stones or small rocks on and around the pegs (see below).

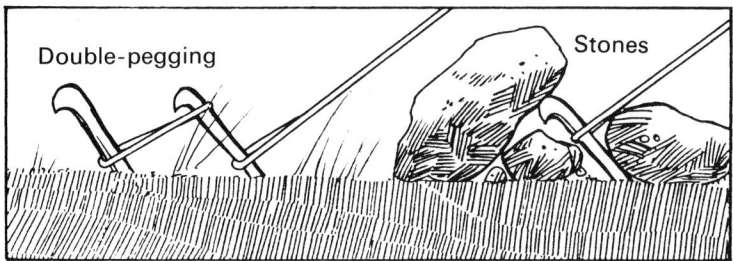

2.4 Making camp—camping methods

When the tents have been pitched, the next step is to cook a meal and then prepare for the night. If you want to check that stream water is clean enough to use for drinking, cooking or washing in, you can look for **stoneflies** on the undersides of the larger stones. If you find some stoneflies, then the water is probably clean. Also, if the water is running freely and you are upstream of any houses, then it should be all right to drink. Always check in case there are any dead animals upstream. If you are not sure about its condition, you can boil the water or use purifying tablets.

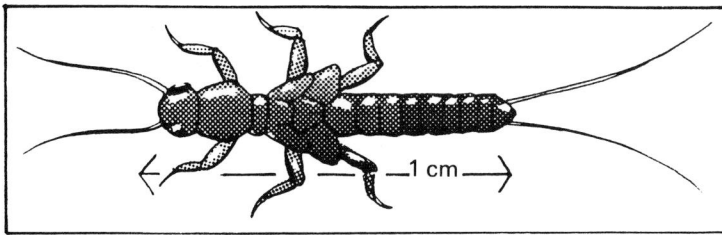

Stoneflies mean the water is clean

It is best to cook in the open rather than inside the tent, but if you are forced to retreat to the shelter of the tent because of bad weather, use your stove near the tent's entrance. This will allow any fumes to escape and you can, if necessary in an emergency, easily throw a flaring stove outside before it sets fire to anything. If you do lose control of your stove, you can smother small fires with a sleeping bag, but if the tent itself is alight, get out immediately.

A tent is a relatively small space in which a great deal of equipment, personal effects and, of course, any number of bodies have to be stored. This well-known phrase is worth remembering:

A place for everything—everything in its place.

In other words, get organised, cut out the chaos and live comfortably! This phrase can also be usefully applied to the camp site as a whole. Here are some important camp site tips:

1 *For comfort*
    Don't wear boots or wet socks inside the tent.
    Change into dry clothes for the night.
    Put spare clothes inside a polythene bag and use this as a pillow.
    Store any unwanted things under the flysheet.
2 *For personal hygiene*
    Wash and clean teeth as normal (use the stream or a lake).
    Wash hands before cooking and after going to the toilet.
    For toilet arrangements, dig a hole, cover with soil and replace turf after use.
3 *For camp cleanliness*
    Store perishable food in a cool place (in the ground or water).
    Wash dishes and pans straight away, don't leave it to the rain or sheep!
    Keep the tent clean inside.

2.5 Striking camp

Packing up to move on, to go to another site or to go home, is called **striking camp**. In the same way that a tent is packed away in reverse, so too, should the camp site be returned to normal. Deal with the little things first. Cooking utensils should be cleaned and personal equipment loaded. Any wet items are best put in polythene bags. Always try to allow damp tents to dry before taking them down. Finally, check that you have not left anything behind, and that the site is in a similar, or better, state to that in which you found it. Try to leave nothing but tent prints.

> *Exercise 10*
> An excellent way of preparing for more challenging things is to plan an overnight camp in the school/college grounds or local wood. The best test of a successful camp is the state of the site afterwards.

3 EXPEDITIONS

For our purposes, the term **expedition** is used to describe a planned walk and camp of one or more nights. To help you to live as comfortably and safely as possible with a minimum amount of equipment, this section includes information on food, particular hazards and suggestions for long distance walks.

3.1 Food for energy

On backpacking expeditions, it is important to have the stamina to be able to keep going for long periods. Your body is often using up a great deal of energy and, in the same way as a car uses petrol, you need to keep your 'tank filled up' by eating and drinking properly. The 'fuel' for your body are the **calories** in food—the more calories you eat, the more energy you have available. Normally, we require about 2–3000 calories a day. However, when carrying a heavy load, such as a rucksack, over long distances in the mountains, this figure goes up to over 4000 calories a day because of the increased amounts of energy being used.

The danger is to be tempted to skimp on food in order to keep the rucksack as light as possible, when really we should be *increasing* our normal food intake by about a quarter. Two hot meals a day (breakfast and dinner) are needed, plus a sensible snack at mid-day and various other high-energy snacks throughout the day, such as chocolate, mint cake, dried fruit, sweets and glucose tablets. Drink, too, is important and necessary in both hot weather, to replace sweat, and in cold weather, as a warm-up.

What is the most suitable food to take with you on a trip or expedition? All foods are made up of varying amounts of **fats**, **proteins** and **carbohydrates**. A good, balanced,

Dehydrated food is lighter to carry

everyday diet should contain all three components. However, foods which are rich in carbohydrates provide more readily-available calories than foods rich in fats or proteins. Therefore when going on trips you should plan to eat plenty of sweet things, bread, potatoes, rice and other high-calorie carbohydrate foods.

Since you have to carry all your food, the weight of it is obviously important. Most foods contain a high percentage of water and if that water is removed (called **dehydrating** the food), the weight of the food can be reduced by up to ninety per cent. The original weight of the food is quickly regained when cooking by simply adding the water to the dehydrated food. Examples of dehydrated or dried foods include: 'quickrice', curry, packet soup, onions, peas, potatoes, noodles, Swiss-style breakfast mixes and powdered milk. All these and more can be found in the local supermarket. You can also buy specialist backpackers' 'ready' meals, which are very light to carry but rather heavy on your pocket! They tend to be expensive. A simple test for choosing foods is: If it cannot be cooked inside 20 minutes in one pan, it's too complicated! On backpacking expeditions of a few days or more, it is likely you will come across a village shop. In fact, it's a good idea to plan for this in order to re-stock supplies. This way, you do not need to carry unnecessary amounts of food.

Points to remember:
1 Dried and dehydrated food is light and easy to carry.
2 The food carried should be easy to cook.
3 Choose food that is high in carbohydrates, for extra energy.
4 Two suitable meals plus lunch and high-energy snacks throughout the day are needed to replace the energy used up.

Exercise 11
Copy the menu sheet below, then fill-in the meals for a weekend camp. Remember the above points and if you can, try out your choice!

MENU SHEET: Weekend Camping Trip	DAY ONE (FRI) ARRIVE AT CAMP	DAY TWO (SAT) MOUNTAIN WALK CAMP	DAY THREE (SUN) STRIKE CAMP
BREAKFAST			
LUNCH			
DINNER			
SUPPER			

CAMPING AND EXPEDITIONS

3.2 Mountain hazards—weather

When planning an expedition it is vital to find out what the weather conditions are likely to be, and to keep yourself up to date with forecasts throughout the trip. British weather is noted for its changeability! Often, it changes dramatically from day-to-day, and in mountain altitudes, a good day can turn into one which produces difficult and potentially-dangerous conditions in a matter of minutes. A basic understanding of '**lows**', '**highs**', wind direction and strength is necessary in order to know what to expect and to be able to plan accordingly. In very remote areas, where help is not close at hand, decisions based on the weather need to be taken sooner rather than later. This may mean having to retreat or taking an escape route well before the storm arrives or reaches full strength.

Don't be caught out by the weather!

The main trouble-makers are rain, cold and wind. On its own, rain is probably the easiest to cope with (by putting on 'cags' and, if necessary, taking shelter). The cold too, in itself, is not too much of a problem. In most cases it can be dealt with by the addition of more clothes, hats, gloves, etc. But when the wind gets up, its strength combined with its coldness (the **wind-chill**) can cause real problems. When combined with rain, all these effects can produce severe conditions.

Where do wind and rain come from? Wind is caused by the movement of air around the world in the form of 'swirls' which go in one direction or another. Most of our weather comes from fast moving, anti-clockwise swirls of air called lows or **depressions**. These are names for areas of low atmospheric pressure, and they usually move across the country from west to east. The direction of the wind in Britain is therefore often from the west or south-west. These winds have passed over the Atlantic Ocean and so hold a lot of water vapour which they have picked up by evaporation. This evaporation eventually forms clouds and brings rain.

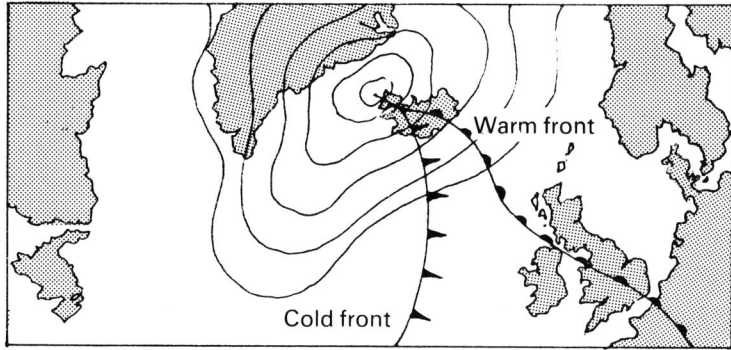

A depression (low) on its way to Britain

The marks which look like thumb prints on weather charts, show depressions. The lines on the chart which join places with the same air pressure are called **isobars**.

When the isobars are close together, the change in pressure is great and this indicates strong winds (in the same way that close contours on a map show steep slopes). In most depressions the rain tends to come from **fronts**. A front is the name given to the boundary between warm and cold air. At these boundaries in a depression, the warm air rises over the cold air and as it does so, it cools down. Cool air cannot hold nearly as much water as warm air and so clouds form and then rain falls. Rain is also caused by air being forced upwards when it blows against mountains or hills. This is why the highest land in Britain is also the wettest.

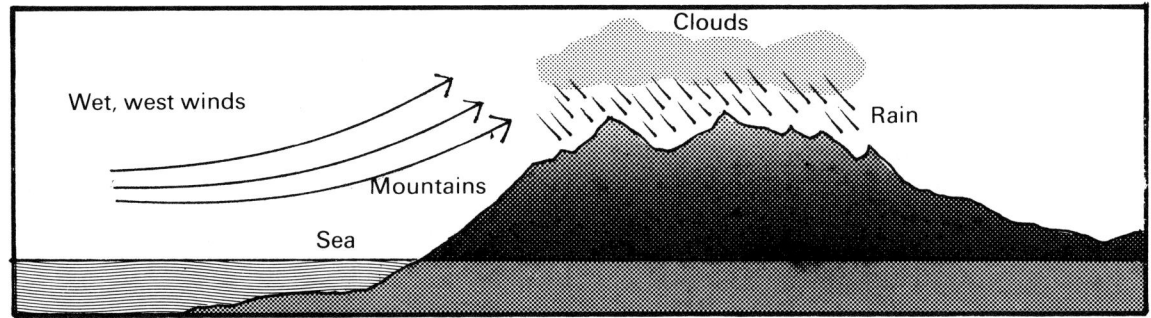
Air forced to rise over mountains cools, forms clouds and produces rain

Summer depressions bring cool, wet and windy—sometimes stormy—weather. Depressions in winter make the air feel milder for the time of year.

Although the British weather is dominated by depressions sweeping in from the west, larger high pressure areas, called highs, from time-to-time manage to nudge their way across from the east or south, bringing more settled, calmer weather and cloudless skies. In summer, this means it is generally warm and dry when we are experiencing 'highs'; in winter, it is cold and frosty but usually also clear and bright.

Sometimes a small area of high pressure called a **ridge** extends between two lows. This brings a short period of settled weather when the wind drops and skies clear.

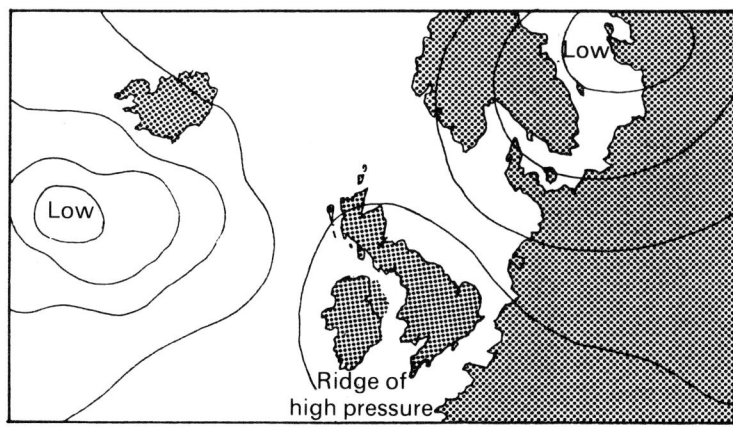
A ridge of high pressure over Britain

Then as the ridge is pushed back by the next low moving in, the clouds, wind and rain return. Britain is often described as a battleground where lows and highs move in and out all through the year. This is why 'British Weather' cannot be relied upon and why it is difficult to forecast.

In the mountains, of course, accurate forecasting is even more of a problem. You should remember that most weather forecasts are based on readings taken at sea-level, and so you need to be aware of two important points:

1 The temperature drops the higher up you go (by as much as 1 °C for every 100 m climbed).
2 The wind speed often increases with height.

However, the weathermen usually *do* get it right, and it is always wise to trust their skill in predicting what is going to happen. You must also try to work out for yourself what is likely to happen in the mountains. Also bear in mind the time-lags between when the readings were taken, when the information was given out and you arriving at your chosen location. Always plan well ahead.

Points to remember:

1 In the mountains the weather can change very quickly.
2 Summer lows, which look like thumb prints on weather maps, bring windy, wet and cool weather—the closer the isobars, the stronger the wind.
3 Summer highs are usually warm, calm and windless.
4 A ridge of high pressure will not last for long.

Exercise 12
1. Collect weather maps from newspapers and record forecasts from the television over a period of a week.
2. At the same time record the actual weather—the wind direction and strength, cloud cover, and what falls from the cloud.
3. Compare the forecasts to what actually happened.

Exercise 13
You are preparing for a weekend expedition. During the week before, work out what the weather will be for each day of the expedition. (Use a card similar to the menu card on page 57.) If necessary change the information as the weekend approaches. Then on Friday morning stick with your final forecast and see if you were right!

Three points to remember when preparing an expedition:
1. Get weather information several days before.
2. Get a local weather forecast when you arrive.
3. Get an up-date on the weather as often as possible during the expedition from a radio, and from other mountaineers you meet.

3.3 Long distance walks

Backpacking expeditions are usually, but not necessarily, associated with some form of **long distance walk**. The Long Distance Walking Association, which has thousands of members, gives this name to any route over 20 miles. Most of the recognised walking routes have names. The most famous is the Pennine Way, and there are well over a hundred other routes throughout Britain. For most of these, guide books are available and new routes are being added each year. Walkers can spend days following these Long Distance Footpaths, many of which pass through some of Britain's most attractive scenery. The Pennine Way, for example, is the longest route in Britain and walking its full length would fill a holiday.

The waymark sign is used in plaque or stencil form by the Countryside Commission on long distance routes.

Exercise 14
To practise your backpacking skills on a recognised route within easy reach of your home:
1. Find out where your nearest Long Distance Path is. Information about all of Britain's paths can be found in: *Long Distance Paths: An International Directory*, by H. D. Westacott (Penguin Books, 1981). This book and other information can be obtained from your local library or information centre.
2. Plan and carry out an expedition on a section of your chosen Long Distance Path.

? FURTHER INFORMATION

The Backpackers' Club *produces a bi-monthly magazine called* Backchat. *For your county coordinator, write to: Hon. National Organiser, 20 St Michaels Road, Tilehurst, Reading, Berks, RG3 4RP.*

The Long Distance Walkers' Association *produces a magazine three times a year, called* Strider. *Information can be obtained from the Secretary, Long Distance Walkers' Association, 8 Upton Grey Court, Winchester, Hants.*

The Camping Club of Great Britain and Ireland *produces a monthly magazine,* Camping and Caravanning. *Their address is 11 Lower Grosvenor Place, London SW1.*

Information about all of Britain's Long Distance Paths can be found in the book by H. D. Westacott (see Exercise 14).

WORKSHEET

1. Explain why a rucksack needs built-in ventilation.

2. It is important to have something under your sleeping bag. Why? What should you use?

3. How would you pitch a tent in the pouring rain?

4. Name three spots to avoid when pitching a tent.

5. What type of weather is associated with a 'thumb-print low'?

6. List five sources of information on weather forecasts.

7. Explain why we need to eat more in the mountains than we would normally.

8. Give examples of the kinds of food you would need for a mountain expedition.

9. What would happen if you were to pump too soon when lighting a primus stove?

10. Explain what can be planned for on an expedition of a few days so that you do not need to carry all your food requirements.

11. Complete the following three sentences, which are useful reminders when putting together weather forecasts for an expedition.
    (a) Get... (b) Get... (c) Get...

12. Describe and draw the sign which shows that you are on a Long Distance Path.

13. List two advantages and two disadvantages of light tents when compared with larger tents.

14. A simple test to remember when choosing food for the mountains is... (Complete).

15. Using the route you planned for your overnight camp in Exercise 7 (Section 2.2):
    (a) Work out the distance.
    (b) Find the compass bearing from the start (687 603) to the finish (663 719).

16. If you had the choice, which of the three types of stove (gas/paraffin/meths) would you take with you? Explain your reasons.

17. STOP–INSULATE–FEED is the procedure for dealing with someone showing signs of mountain hypothermia. What additional pieces of equipment would you have on a backpacking expedition to help you insulate him or her, and how would you use them?

18. In Section 2.2, we discovered there are five essentials to bear in mind when choosing a camp site.
    (a) List these in order, putting what you think is the most important first and the least important last.
    (b) Add anything else you can think of to make this your 'ideal site'.

19. Write a paragraph on 'Living in a tent.' Base your answer on a group of three sharing a tent, and include an explanation of how the jobs would be divided up.

20. Design a poster for backpackers with the title: LEAVE NOTHING BUT TENT PRINTS.

4 ORIENTEERING

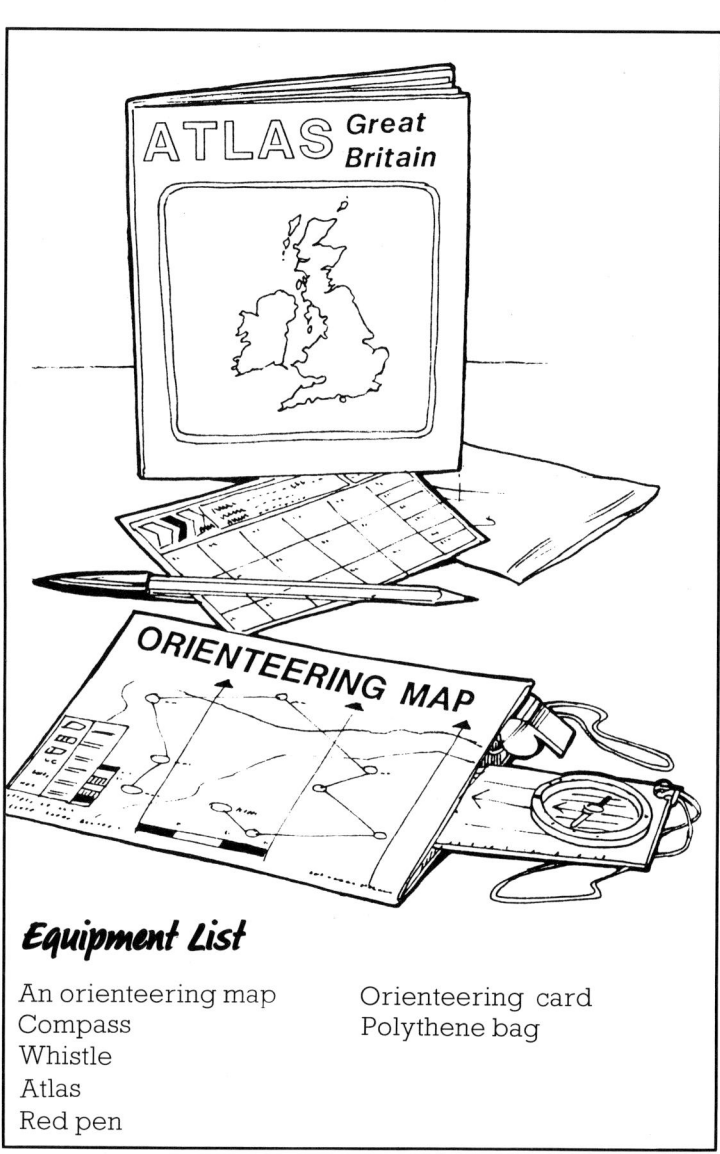

Equipment List

An orienteering map
Compass
Whistle
Atlas
Red pen

Orienteering card
Polythene bag

Introduction

You may think orienteering is a strange name for a sport, but basically, all it means is 'moving around' and 'finding the way'.

Moving around what? Well, orienteering usually takes place in forests, woods and rough open land, although streets, school fields and parks are also used, in the day as well as at night.

Finding the way where, and how? Everyone taking part is given a special map of the forest, or wherever. It shows where a number of markers have been placed. The markers are called **controls**. Using the map and a compass, the idea is to find each control in a given order and to reach the finish as quickly as possible. It's as simple as that!

The first part of this Chapter expands this simple definition of the sport to include its origins, where and how it developed, and how orienteering is organised in Britain. It also explains how to get in touch with your local orienteering club.

In Section 2, the skills which you will eventually take with you to an orienteering event are developed. This includes tips and hints on how to use clues from the map for route selection, judging distances and generally finding the way. By the time you have read the third Section, you should be ready to compete in an orienteering event organised by a local club.

63

1 WHAT IS ORIENTEERING?

Orienteering is a very popular and highly organised sport. In Britain, there are many clubs which hold events and competitions throughout the year. But just what exactly do orienteers do?

1.1 About the sport

Orienteering involves completing a course by finding your way to and between the controls, which are marked on the special orienteering map as circles. You must do this in the shortest possible time, using a combination of cross-country running and map reading skills.

It is not a treasure hunt. The controls are not hidden—they are in fairly easy places to find. Orienteering is therefore mainly a test of your ability to select the best and quickest **route** between the controls. This does not always mean sprinting along the shortest distance to the next control, because the shortest distance may take you through very difficult terrain, such as thick forest or up steep slopes. Often, it is best to take longer but safer routes, such as easy to follow paths or tracks where the chances of getting lost and losing time are very much more reduced.

Some people try to run as fast as possible, not spending time to check the route on the map properly, and so they tend to get lost easily. Others go slowly, always knowing exactly where they are, and carefully checking the route all the time. They often finish more quickly than those who try to go very fast. Most orienteers, however, try to combine both these approaches by running along the easy to follow sections, and going slowly and carefully along the difficult sections, or avoiding these completely if possible.

Controls are shown as circles on the map but what do they look like on the ground?

At a control point there will be some sort of marker, coloured with red (or orange) and white triangles. The marker will have a coded letter or number on it to identify it as the one you are looking for, and, in proper orienteering events, there will be a **needle punch** hanging from it. On finding the correct control point, you punch your card to prove you have been there, and then plan your route to the next control.

Read the map before setting off—it's quicker in the long run!

ABOUT THE SPORT

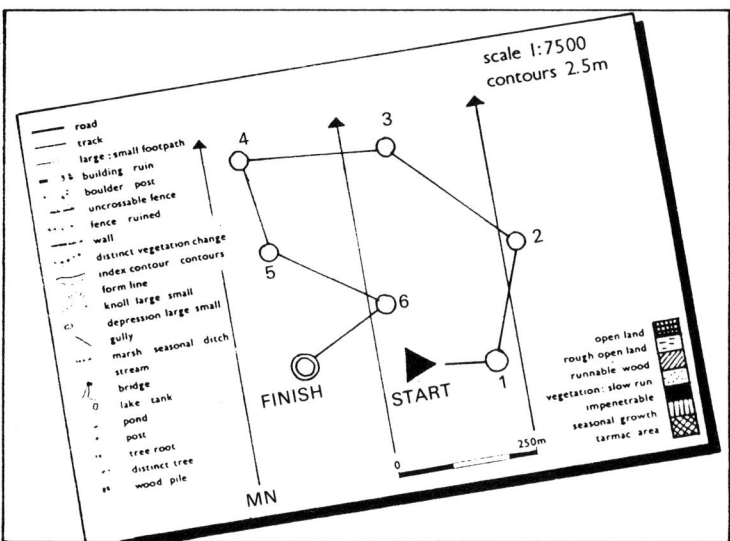

An orienteering map shows the control points as circles

Punch your card at a control point

In addition to the map, the equipment you need, at least to start with, includes:
1. a whistle (to use in case you get lost or injured)
2. a polythene bag (to hold and protect your map and card)
3. a red pen (to draw the circles onto your map at the start of the event, if they are not marked on already)
4. a compass (useful to help you set the map. Setting the map is discussed in Chapter 1, Section 1.6.)
5. clothing (to cover and protect your arms and legs from scratches).

However, like other sports, there is a range of specialist clothing and equipment available for keen orienteers. Such clothing and equipment includes:
1. lightweight nylon suits
2. 'Bramble Bashers' (rubberised or plastic-fronted long socks to protect legs from brambles)
3. orienteering shoes (which have studded soles for extra grip)
4. compasses which strap onto the hand (such as Type II Silva or the Suunto 'Handy').

Orienteering events attract all sorts of people—individuals, groups and families of all ages, both male and female, who either belong to a club or simply turn up on the day to enjoy a run or walk in the countryside.

Competitors are usually split into classes depending upon their sex and age. A wide age range is usually represented—from under 10 to over 56. You need not compete on your own if you don't want to: pairs and threesomes are not unusual.

Exercise 1

Complete the following sentences to form a paragraph with the title: *The Sport of Orienteering*.
1. Orienteering is a sport which takes place in . . . .
2. Each competitor has a map which shows . . . .
3. The idea is to . . . .
4. It is mainly a test of . . . .
5. To prove that you have been to each control point, ...
6. It is a sport for everyone because . . . .

1.2 Orienteering history

Orienteering originated as a military training activity in the vast forests of Scandinavia (Norway, Sweden and Finland) in the 1890s. In 1918, Major Ernst Killander developed the activity into a sport in order to encourage youngsters to make use of the forests of Sweden. He called it 'Orientation'. The word 'Orienteering' was first used by another Swede, Bjorn Kjellstrom, in 1946 (who, with his brothers, also invented the Silva Compass). Orienteering became the sport's official title as it spread from Europe to all parts of the world.

In 1987, the governing body of the sport—the International Orienteering Federation (IOF)—had 32 member nations from countries as wide apart as Australia, North America and Japan. It remains a major sport in the Scandinavian countries, where it is as popular as athletics in this country. The five-day Swedish 'O Ringen' event, for example, has more people taking part in it than compete in the Olympic Games.

The first World Orienteering Championships were held in 1966 in Finland, and are staged every two years in a different member country. In 1976, it was Britain's turn and the event was staged near Aviemore, in Scotland, in the forests of Darnaway and Culbin.

In 1979 the Championships were moved from even-numbered years to odd, to avoid clashes with the Olympic Games. Then in 1985, for the first time ever, they were held outside Europe—in Australia. Even so, all the world titles went to Scandinavians, who still dominate the sport.

> *Exercise 2*
> Draw a map of Europe and mark on it the countries where orienteering started.

Orienteering is steadily growing in popularity

1.3 Orienteering in Britain

The sport came to Britain in 1962 when the Scottish Orienteering Federation was formed. This was followed, in 1965, by the English Orienteering Association (EOA). Then in 1967 both groups joined with Wales and Northern Ireland to form the British Orienteering Federation (BOF). The BOF is the governing body of the sport in Britain (rather like the FA is to soccer) and it is responsible for fixtures, finance and training, and ensures that the rules and events are the same throughout the Federation's twelve Regional Associations.

In the twenty years in which the BOF has been active, the number of events and people taking part has grown steadily with, at present, over 13 000 members and 150 clubs. In 1985 for example, more than 1000 events were held up and down the country, with a total of 180 000 orienteers taking part. Most events are held on Sunday mornings and the main season runs from October to June.

It is usual for about 50 people to take part in small club events, but this number can rise to over 3000 at the two top competitions of the season. These are the British Championships, held at the end of the season in May or June, and the Jan Kjellstrom Trophy, which takes place for two days every Easter, and attracts many orienteers from other countries.

Exercise 3
Find out which orienteering region you live in (use the map alongside). Using the address given at the end of this Chapter, write to BOF for the following information:
1 Details about orienteering.
2 Orienteering clubs in your region, and the nearest one to you.
3 A fixture list of events.

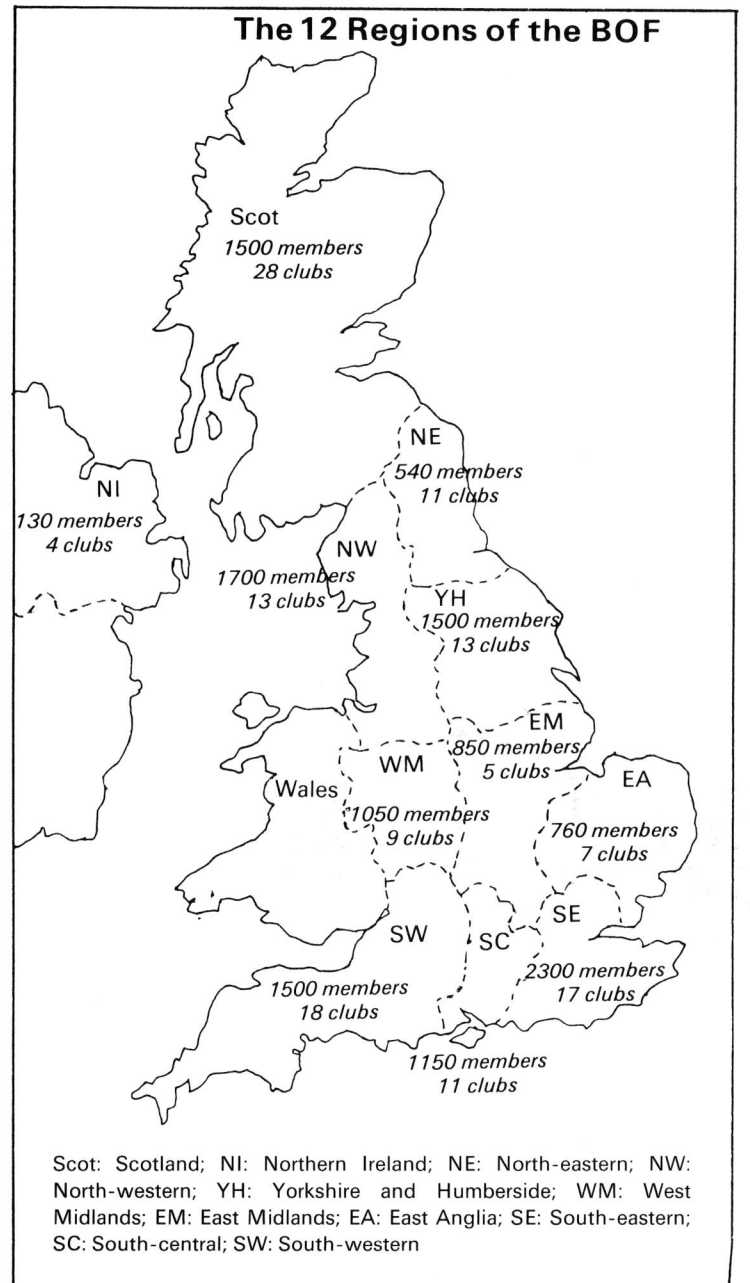

Scot: Scotland; NI: Northern Ireland; NE: North-eastern; NW: North-western; YH: Yorkshire and Humberside; WM: West Midlands; EM: East Midlands; EA: East Anglia; SE: South-eastern; SC: South-central; SW: South-western

2 HOW TO ORIENTEER

Your ability to orienteer really depends on how well you read and use the map to find the way from the start to each control, in the correct order, and then on to the finish. This Section includes ideas and tips on how to do this. You will see that you must, at all times, know where you are.

2.1 The map

Orienteering is about map reading. However an orienteering map is different from an OS map. OS maps are excellent for large areas but they do not give nearly enough information about smaller pieces of land, such as the particular terrain inside an individual forest, and this information is needed for orienteering. A special, larger-scale map is therefore used in order to provide very

ORIENTEERING

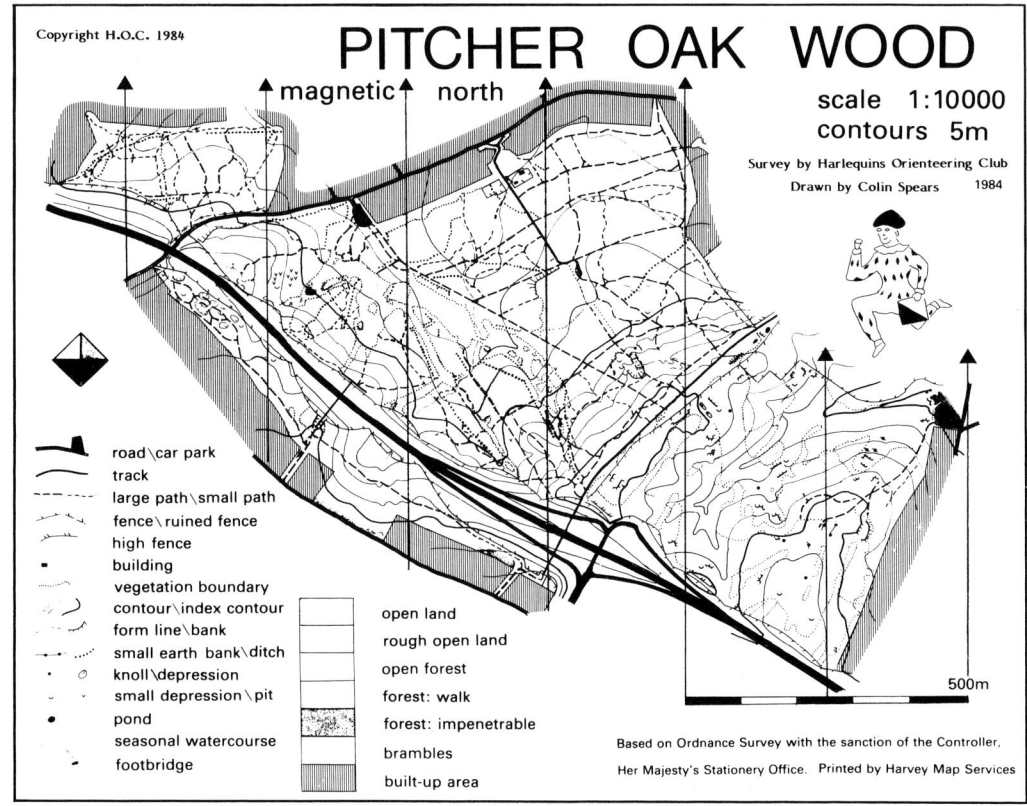

An orienteering map shows much more detail than an OS map

detailed information about such features as ditches, small paths, walls, fences, trees and, most important for the orienteer, the 'runability' and thickness of a forest or wood. Therefore, to give as full and accurate a picture as possible about such small areas, orienteering maps are very carefully surveyed and specially drawn at the following scales:

    1:20 000 – where 1 cm = 200 m
    1:15 000 – where 1 cm = 150 m
    1:10 000 – where 1 cm = 100 m
and 1:5000   – where 1 cm = 50 m

Apart from scale, three other differences are:
1 Orienteering maps are no more than 30 cm long so that they are small enough to hold in one hand.
2 There are no grid lines but there are **magnetic north** lines, which make it easier to set the map with a compass.
3 The IOF symbols are not the same as OS symbols. IOF symbols show four main groups of features, as shown in the following table.

As you can see from the table, the thickness of the vegetation is indicated on the map. This will help you to decide which areas are good or not so good for running or walking. For example, open areas are coloured yellow, runable forest white, and thick forest green (thick forest is also called 'fight' for obvious reasons). Brown features show the shape of the land, including contours at 5 m

HOW TO ORIENTEER

Type of feature	Colour	Example
1 Man-made	Black	Building
2 Water	Blue	Stream
3 Land	Brown	Ditch
4 Vegetation	Yellow	Open land
	White	'Runable' wood
	Green	Thicker wood

IOF map symbols

intervals, small hollows (called **depressions**) and mounds (**knolls**). Water is shown as blue and black indicates man-made features.

All this information and colour may make the orienteering map seem complicated, but when you get used to it, it becomes very clear and fairly easy to read. It is designed to give you the information you need to help you find out exactly where you are, and to decide on the best possible way to go next.

Exercise 4

To become familiar with the symbols used on an orienteering map, draw an imaginary map of a small forest area. Include on it all the features and colours shown in the table above so that there are tracks, paths (small and large), streams, ditches, knolls, depressions and changes in vegetation.

Exercise 5

After finding your nearest orienteering club (Exercise 3), write or telephone for information on local woods/forests or parks which have been specially mapped for orienteering events. They will be pleased to provide this for a small fee.

Get a selection of maps (probably 25 p per copy) and go for walks around the areas they cover to get used to the symbols. Most maps will not have any control points marked on (this is usually done at the time of an event) but you may be able to get hold of some which have been pre-marked to let you see the kinds of places used for siting controls.

Local clubs will also have information on **permanent wayfaring** courses, which have been set up by the BOF, Forestry Commission and local councils in woods and parks all over the country. These have permanent wooden control posts and maps can usually be obtained from Rangers' offices, etc.

Exercise 6 — Map drawing

Based on your new knowledge of orienteering maps, draw as accurate a map as possible of either your school field or a nearby park or wood. Follow the steps below.

1 Use a photocopy of the relevant 1:10 000 OS map as a base. (Copies available from local planning office or OS — address at the end of this Chapter).
2 Check and add the major features — roads, tracks, walls, streams, buildings.
3 Divide the area into sections and survey each section in detail, not forgetting the 'runability' and any changes in vegetation.
4 Collect all the information together to produce a black and white map to use for orienteering practices.

ORIENTEERING

2.2 Knowing where you are

From the moment you start and until you finish an orienteering event, you should know whereabouts on the course you are. This is achieved by continuously looking at and checking your map, and by keeping your map 'set', i.e. hold the map the same way round as the land ahead of you. There are two straightforward ways of setting your map.

1 Identify a few features on the land. Find them on the map, and then turn the map round if necessary, so that it shows the relative positions of the features correctly. (This method is described in Chapter 1, Section 1.6.)
2 A quick way is to use a compass as follows:
 (a) Put the compass on the map any way up.
 (b) Turn both map and compass round until the red end of the compass needle is parallel to the magnetic north lines on the map and pointing to the *top* of the map (see Chapter 1, Section 3.2).

When you have set the map, the features on it should be in line with the same features on the ground, so that when looking down a path, for example, a left-hand turn ahead of you is also a left-hand turn on the map. Remember that you do not need to hold the map with the writing at the top the correct way up. You turn the map around to correspond to the direction in which you are looking.

Thumbing will help you to keep track of where you are as you move about on the course. Keep the thumb of the hand that holds your map close to your position and move it as you run or walk along. Some orienteers even mark an arrow on their thumb nail or colour it to help them.

Set your map using land features

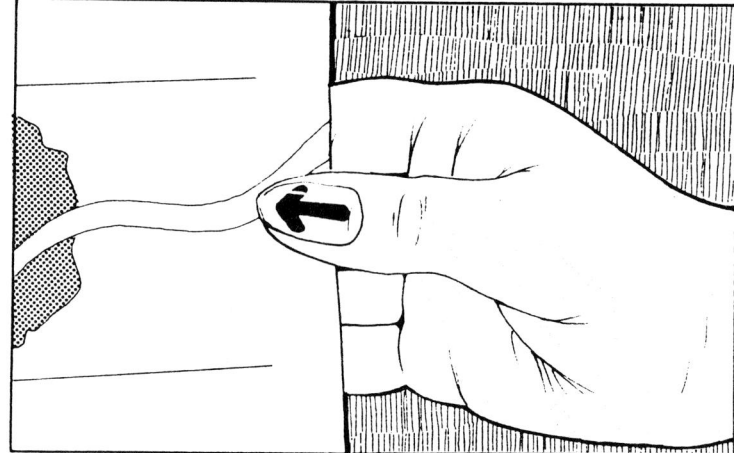

Thumbing is a useful way of keeping track of your position

What do you do if you are not sure where you are? The first sensible thing to do is to *stop*, before you get even more lost! Next, try to recognise the surrounding features. If you can't recognise anything, then you should do one of two things:
1 retrace your steps to a place that you *can* recognise and set the map from there;

or

2 if you are not even sure where you came from, don't hang around; set the map, select a long feature (something you cannot miss, such as a road or track) which is on a simple bearing (e.g. due South) and get there as quickly as you can. On the way, keep looking for anything which might help you locate your position on the map. This method is often much quicker than wandering around aimlessly, hoping to eventually get onto the right track. Using the orienteering map on page 68, for example, no matter where you are, by setting the map and moving due south you will hit the road or track at some point.

Points to remember:
1 Always keep the map set.
2 Always know where you are.
3 Use your thumb to keep track of your position.
4 If you do get lost, stop and act quickly.

Exercise 7—'Follow the leader'
Using a local orienteering map (obtained in Exercise 5) go to the area and take it in turns to lead the group to a specific place 100–200 m away. This tests your ability to choose and follow a route and also to follow someone else's.

Exercise 8
On the map drawn in Exercise 6, change the grid lines to magnetic north lines as follows.
1 Find the magnetic variation of the base map being used (see Section 3.1, Chapter 1).
2 Subtract the magnetic variation from 360 and set this bearing on your compass (e.g. if the magnetic variation is 6° west, turn the housing so that 354° is on the bearing line).
3 Place the compass on the map so that the orienting lines are parallel to the grid lines, and draw a line along the side of the compass (as shown in the diagram below).

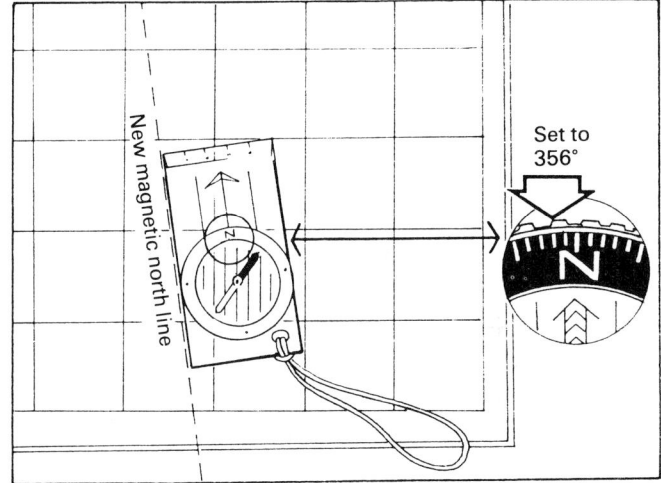

4 Draw a series of parallel MN (magnetic north) lines across your map, 2.5 cm apart (the distance between two lines represents 250 m).
5 Erase the old grid lines.

These MN lines provide a rough indication of the direction of the magnetic pole, and enable you to set the map without adding or subtracting the magnetic variation.

ORIENTEERING

2.3 Choosing your route

Once you know where you are and where you want to go, you must choose the route that you will take. At first, choosing a route might sound like a simple, straightforward business. But in fact, this is the most important part of orienteering and it requires a lot of thought.

Choosing the right route for *you* will depend upon your own experience, knowledge and fitness level. The route that someone else takes may not suit you: they may be more or less fit or experienced than you are. Taking the best route could make the difference between completing the course in a fast or a slow time; or even between competing the course successfully or getting lost!

The first simple choice gives you two options:
1. To run direct to the control, ignoring paths, etc. You would travel 'as the crow flies'.
2. To plan the route using land features such as paths, river banks, etc. which will help you to stay on the right track.

Even though it may be tempting to use the first, inexperienced orienteers should always use the *second* method of route selection, using land features. The most useful features to us are those which are easy to locate and follow both on the map and on the ground. These are called **line features** and include paths, walls, tracks and streams. Try to include as many line features as possible in your route.

On courses designed for beginners, the controls are often placed either on or quite close to a line feature to help with route finding, but you will probably need to use more than one line feature to get from one control to the next. In the diagram below, for instance, although the direct route between the two controls looks to be quicker, it is best to use the first line feature (the track) and then turn left at the footbridge along the second feature (the path). By doing this, the dangers of getting lost or missing the control altogether are virtually non-existent.

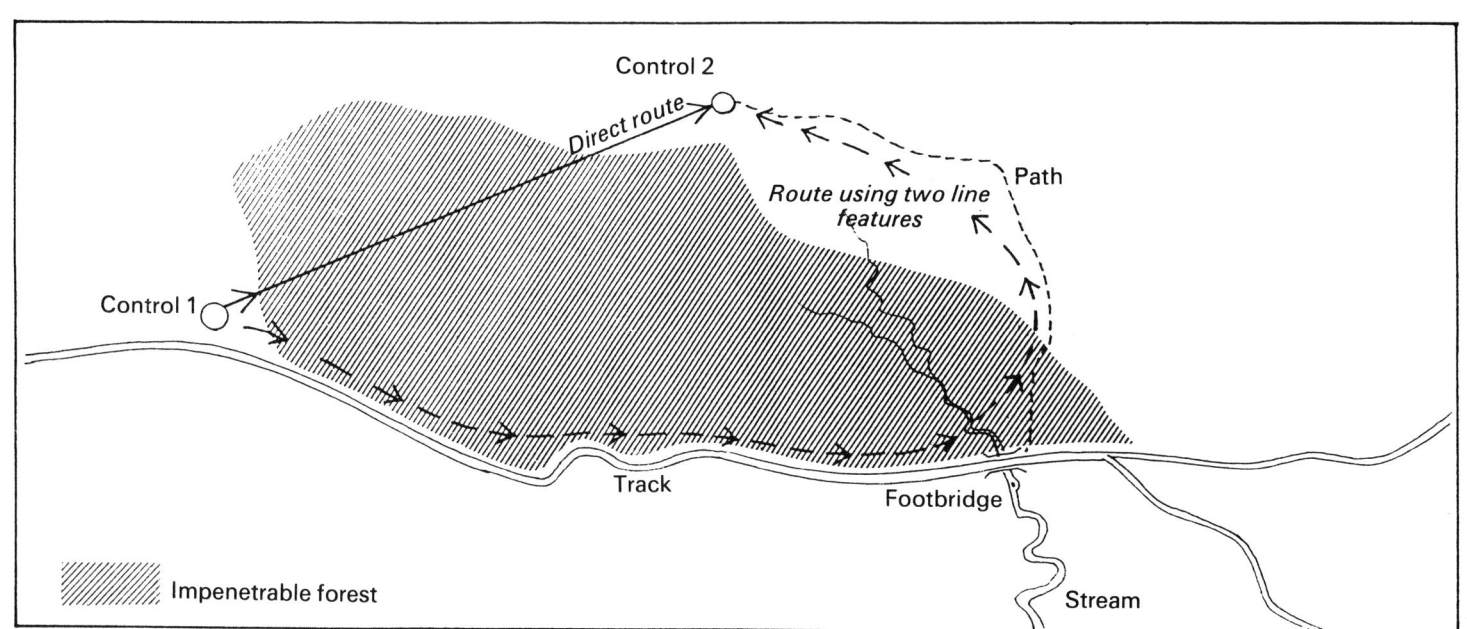

Use line features to choose your route

HOW TO ORIENTEER

When a control is not located on a line feature you should again choose a route using a line feature, and aim to get as close to the control as possible. From this point, you must then plan your final attack on the control. The point that you reach on the line feature is therefore called the **attack point**. The attack point in the following diagram is the junction of paths—it is an easy spot to make for, using the larger path as the line feature.

Using the diagram below, the sequence of movement from control 2 to control 3 would be as follows:
1 Thumb and run along the path to the junction of paths—the attack point.
2 Turn left and carefully follow the small path until you reach the ditch, then turn right.
3 Follow the ditch until you come to the control.

Before leaving an attack point it is good practice to look for a **catching feature**. This is a very distinctive feature, such as a track or stream, beyond the next control and which can be reached in case you miss the control altogether. If you do miss, it is always better to go on to a catching feature from where you can then set the map and aim again than to wander around in the hope of eventually stumbling on the position of the control. The stream and depression in the diagram would make good catching features.

Points to remember:
1 Stay on line features and avoid choosing cross-country routes.
2 Make use of an attack point which is easy to find and close to the control.
3 On reaching the attack point, stop and plan your final move.
4 Decide on one or several catching features.
5 If you think you have missed the control, go on to the catching feature and plan again.

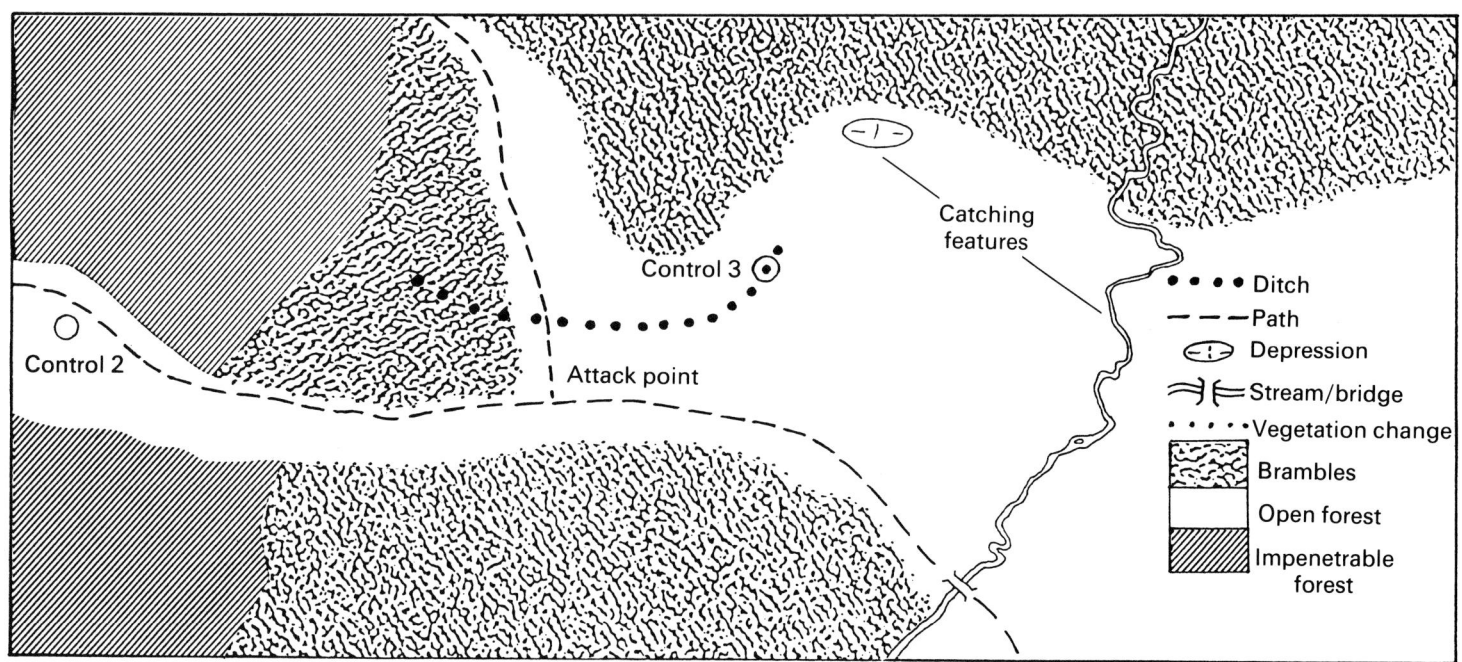

Learn to use line features, attack points and catching features

ORIENTEERING

Exercise 9—Choosing a route
Using a map which contains pre-marked controls (obtained in Exercise 5) decide on and write down your route between the controls in the following way.

ROUTE	Line feature to attack point	Final Route	Catching feature
START –1	Run down large path on a bearing of 120° until reaching the bridge then turn left to the lake.	From the lake, follow the stream to the ditch	Track 100 m beyond ditch
1–2	From ditch, move on to path and run until reaching second path on right.	Take turning on right, follow bank to control	Pond

2.4 How far?

Sometimes, knowing where you are and which way to go is not enough, and it becomes important to be able to work out *how far* along a path you need to run or walk. You can judge distance in two ways:

1. Using the map scales on the compass. In the following map diagram, the length of the path, from the junction to the attack point, is 400 m (scale 1:10 000; 1 cm ≡ 100 m, so 4 cm ≡ 400 m). You may find that knowing the distance is all the information you need in order to help you to judge how far to go, but if knowing that you have to run or walk 400 m means nothing to you, use the second method.

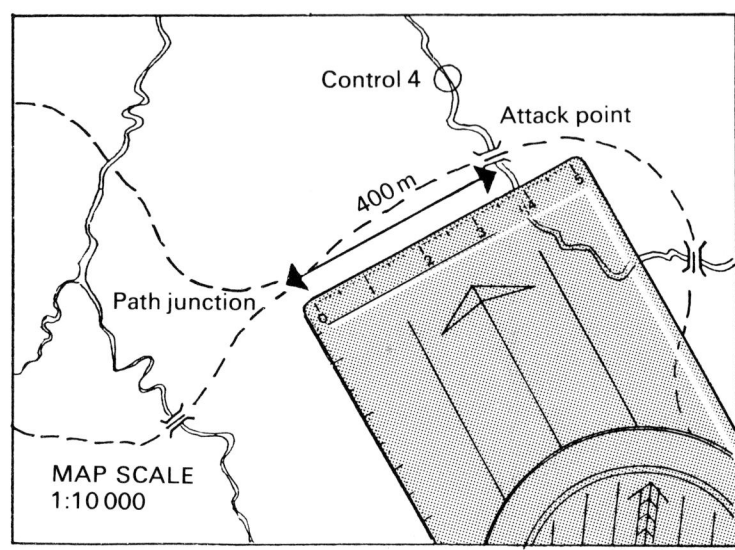

Using the compass ruler to find the distance

2. **Pacing** can be used to judge how much distance you have covered. In order to use this technique, you must first know how many **double paces** you take to cover 100 m. (You count a double pace by counting every time one of your feet hits the ground. This is easier than counting every single pace. It doesn't matter which foot you choose to count on, but it must be the same one each time!) Once you have worked out how many paces you take to cover 100 m, you can easily apply the same technique to other distances. So, assume that your double pacing count for 100 m is 40. The distance you need to cover is 400 m (4 × 100 m), so your double pacing count would be 4 × 40 = 160 counts. Some orienteers construct a small scale on a piece of tape which they then stick onto their compass. Working out how many paces to take then becomes a simple matter of reading the value off the tape when the edge of the compass is held alongside the distance to be covered on the map.

HOW TO ORIENTEER

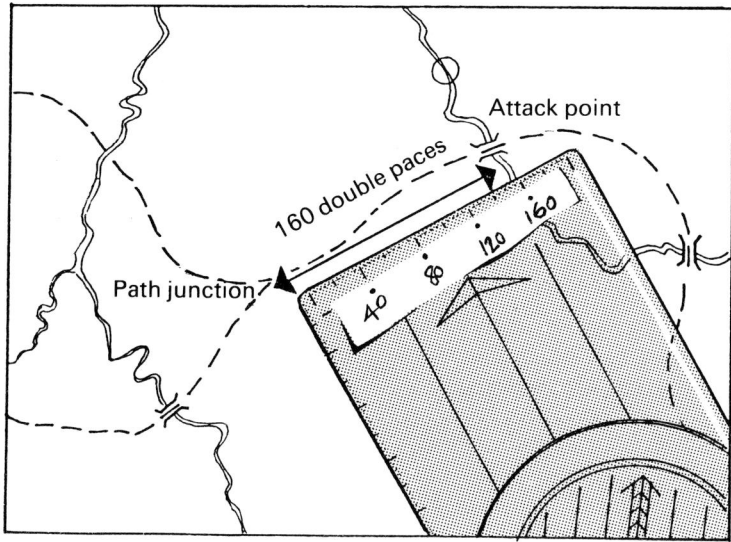

A double-pace scale provides a useful measure of distance

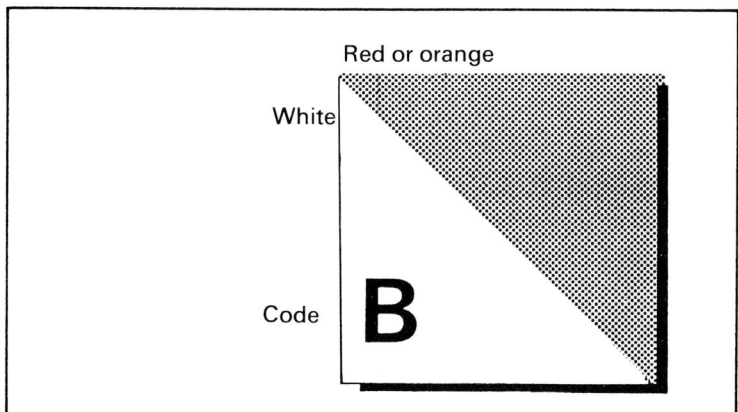

This is what you will find at a control point

Exercise 10
Work out your double pace count for a distance of 100 m on a path.
1 Measure and mark off 100 m, or use an athletics track.
2 Run at an easy, comfortable pace and count every time your left (or right) foot hits the ground.
3 Do this four or five times and take the average.
Also try this on rough ground, bracken or long grass and compare the results.

Exercise 11 — An orienteering competition
In small groups, take it in turns to plan a course using either the orienteering map drawn in Exercise 6, or a map of a local wood. You require:
1 Maps of the area.
2 Six to eight control markers, made from card or wood, each one with the orienteering sign (red and white triangles) and a different code.
3 A card for each competitor which will give the following information:
 —name
 —time out/in
 —a space to write down the code at each control
4 A sheet for each competitor which has a brief description of where to find each control, e.g. 'On a post in the corner of the field'.

Remember these points:
1 Position the controls on line features.
2 Do not hide the controls!
3 Set competitors off at one minute intervals, not all together.

3 AN ORIENTEERING EVENT

Now that you have found out what orienteering is all about, and have made contact with your local club, it is time to take part in a real, properly organised event. This Section introduces you to the different types of orienteering available and gives guidance about what to do at an event organised by an orienteering club.

3.1 What to do

Orienteering events are organised by members of local clubs and normally take place on Sunday mornings, usually at all times throughout the year. Once in contact with a club, you will be sent information about where events are due to be held and also the phone numbers of the organisers, who will be pleased to tell you more about where to meet (usually a car park near a wood), the courses on offer, the time, the cost and the scale of map to be used.

There may be no need to book or fill in any entry forms beforehand—you can often simply turn up on the day. Events with age classes, however, usually *do* require you to enter before the day, so that each competitor can be provided with a pre-bagged, pre-marked map.

What do you need to take?

You need the following:
1 suitable clothes (see Section 1.1)
2 a red pen (to mark-in the position of the controls)
3 a polythene bag or map case
4 a whistle
5 a compass
6 some money (usually about 50p to cover the cost of the map and contribute towards the organisation).

Where do you go when you get there?

On reaching the car park, the first thing to do is to report to the Registration Point. This is usually a car, or group of cars, each with different lengths of courses displayed on their windscreens. You decide on which course to do (more of this in the next Section). Then you go to the window of that car and pay the entry fee. The registrar will ask you when you would like to start. Choose a starting time which will give you a chance to walk to the Start and prepare yourself properly.

You will then be given:
1 the map
2 a **description sheet**—this lists all the controls on your chosen course, it tells you where they are located and gives an identification number for each one. The card below shows that control number 1 can be found on the east side of the pond, and that its identifying number is 87. By checking the identification number, you can be sure you have reached the correct control.

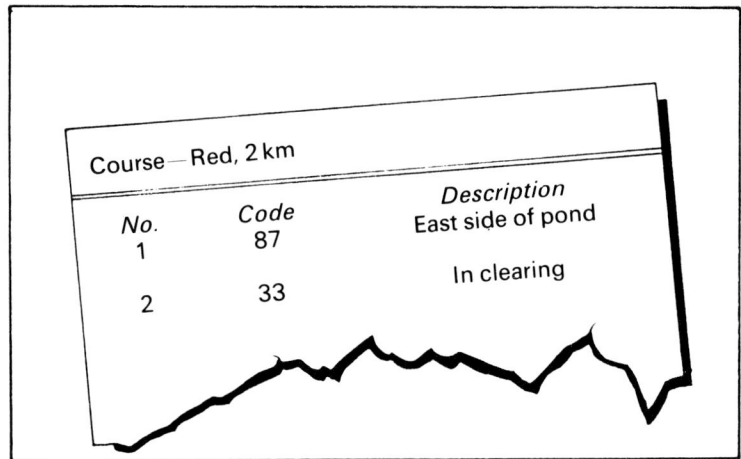

3 a **control card**. This has two sections, the larger part, which is carried with you, and the stub, which is handed in at the Start. The larger part has a number of boxes drawn on it. Each of these boxes must be punched at the appropriate control point.

All the above items (map, description sheet and control card) should be put into a polythene bag to keep them safe and clean.

AN ORIENTEERING EVENT

A control card and stub

Age	Class
10 and under	M10, W10
11–12	M11, W11
13–14	M13, W13
15–16	M15, W15
17–18	M17, W17
19–20	M19
21–34	M21
19–34	W19
35–42	M35, W35
43–49	M43, W43
50–55	M50, W50
56 and over	M56, W56

M = men/boys   W = women/girls

How do you begin?

The Start is normally a little way from the Registration Point but it will be clearly marked. On the way (and while you are waiting to begin) spend the time studying the map. Find out where you are, look for line features and see if there are any other major features which may help you find your way between controls.

Three minutes before your start time, you will be called and asked to make your way to the **pre-start**. This is where you hand in your control card stub. As each minute passes, a whistle is blown and you move up a queue, getting closer to the start line. Alongside you will be other orienteers who will have the same starting time, but who will be doing different courses. Then it's off! But where?

If your map has not been pre-marked with control points, and this is usual in local events, you need to make your way to the **master maps**, a short distance away. These have the courses marked on them and you must carefully copy down the positions of the controls using a red pen (red because it does not clash with the other colours on the map). Work quickly but accurately.

After you have done this, set your map, choose a safe route to the first control, and set off fairly slowly to give you a chance to get used to things.

Copying details from the master map

77

ORIENTEERING

How can you be sure you have found the correct control?

The control marker below is located on the east side of a pond and has the code number 87 on it (as described on page 76). It is the **code** that tells you that you have found the right control.

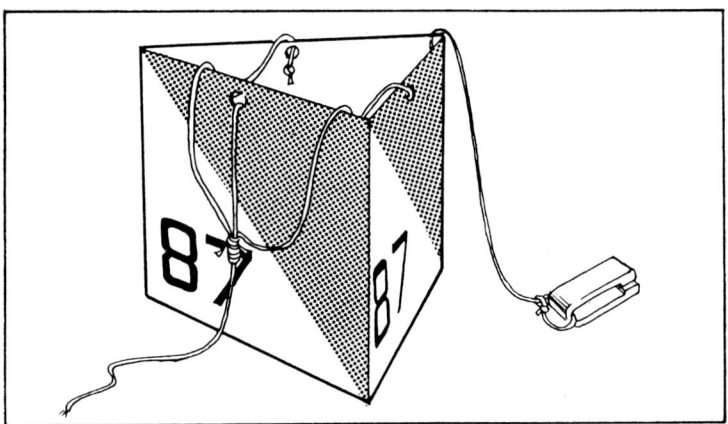

What to do to prove you have been there

By the side of each control, or hanging from it, is a punch (see below). You must punch the appropriate box on your control card—for control number 1, punch box 1, and so on. All these are checked at the end, and, since each punch leaves a different pattern, it is proof that you have indeed visited all the control points.

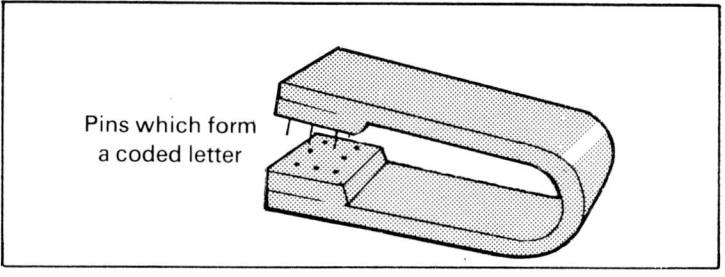

What to do at the final control

The route from the last control to the finish is marked. So run fast, and hand in your control card to the official who will record your finishing time on it and keep it to check that it is complete and correct. Then its back to the car park for a cup of squash—which is free!

How do you find out how well you have done?

Throughout the morning, the control card stubs of the orienteers who have finished are stapled in order of time onto a string. Although the control cards themselves have not yet been checked, this gives an initial idea of how well each competitor has done. For a list of the complete results (and the date of the next event) you should leave a stamped addressed envelope in the box which is usually marked 'Results'. You should get a reply a week to ten days later.

3.2 Which course?

Orienteering courses vary in length and difficulty, ranging from 2 km courses with 6–10 easy-to-find controls for beginners or young competitors, to courses of 7.5 km or more, where route finding is hard. At all events there are at least three courses on offer, and usually more. At most local and open events a colour-coded system is used: the courses are given colours which indicate the length and difficulty. The colours range from white, which is for beginners, to brown, for the very experienced competitors.

The idea is to move up a colour when you feel you are ready to, as your skills improve. However, it's important not to go for a course which is too difficult too soon. Many people have been put off the sport because they failed to understand the differences between the courses, and ended up choosing one that was unsuitable. Not surprisingly, they got lost!

AN ORIENTEERING EVENT

Colour of course	Difficulty	Experience needed	Length of course	Average time	Position of controls	Choice of routes
White	V. easy	Beginners	1–1.5 km	20 min	On line features (e.g. path junctions)	No route choice
Yellow	Easy		1.5–2 km	30 min		
Orange	Easy/moderate	Inexperienced	2.5–3.5 km	45 min	Near line features	Simple route choice
Red	Moderate		4.5–6 km	60 min		
Green	Hard	Only experienced orienteers	3.5–4.5 km	50 min	Away from line features; no obvious attack points	Plenty of route choice
Blue			5.5–7 km	60 min		
Brown			7 km +	70 min		

Colour codes of courses

Exercise 12—An orienteering event
Try out your skills and knowledge at a local event. Obtain a fixture list from a local club and choose an event. Prepare yourself beforehand and remember the following points.
1 Check the ages for the different classes.
2 Check the courses available, and choose the easiest.
3 Decide whether to run on your own or with someone else—either is allowed.
4 Know what to take and what to do once you are there.
5 Keep your map afterwards.

Exercise 13—After the event
1 Repeat Exercise 9 (choosing a route) but this time use the map from the event you went to, and the routes you took between the controls.
2 Discuss, in a group, the routes taken and decide on good and not-so-good choices.

Conclusion

One of the original reasons behind the development of this sport in the forests of Scandinavia was to give people the chance to get out into the countryside. This remains true today. Orienteering has grown into a sport with something for everyone—for individuals, athletes, the young and old, male and female, for families and friends. It offers an interesting and exciting way of getting and keeping fit, using a minimum of equipment and giving maximum amounts of enjoyment. Provided you remember that the map is the most important piece of equipment and it is your ability to read it that is being tested, you, too, should be able to get some pleasure from the sport.
GOOD LUCK!

? FURTHER INFORMATION

Equipment

Silva Compasses (UK) Ltd, PO Box 15, Feltham, Middlesex, TW13 6DF   Tel: 01 898 6901.

Suunto Compasses (including the new 'JES' compass): Newbold and Bulford Ltd, Enbecco House, Carlton Park, Saxmundham, Suffolk, IP17 2NL Tel: 0728 2933.

Computer Software

'The Forest'—a computer simulation of orienteering. Available for 48K Sinclair ZX Spectrum (from Phipps Associates, Dept 5, Freepost EM 463. Tel: 03727 21215) and the complete BBC range from Model B to Archimedes (from Cunning Running Software, 11 Avon Buildings, Flower Lane, Amesbury, Wilts SP4 7HF, Tel: 0908 22369).

Maps

It is all right to photocopy parts of OS maps if your educational establishment is supported by LEA. If not, permission can be obtained from: Ordnance Survey, Romsey Road, Maybush, Southampton SO9 4DH   Tel: 0703 792000

Addresses

British Orienteering Federation. For a variety of books, slides, videos and information about everything to do with the sport, write to BOF, 'Riversdale', Dale Road North, Darley Dale, Matlock, Derbyshire, DE4 2JB.
The BOF produce a bi-monthly magazine, Compass Sport.

Irish Orienteering Association. Write for details to: Hon. Sec., 111 Haddington Road, Ballsbridge, Dublin 4.

WORKSHEET

1. Draw the orienteering control sign using the correct colours.
2. What do the initials BOF and IOF mean?
3. How are controls marked on a map?
4. List the equipment needed to begin orienteering.
5. Describe the specialist clothing that is available.
6. Although events are held throughout the year, when is the main season for orienteering?
7. What is 'fight'?
8. How can a line feature be of use?
9. Explain, with a drawing, how to use an attack point and a catching feature.
10. What is your double pace for 100 m, 250 m and 400 m?
11. Explain how to set a map using a compass.
12. There are three points which help you to know where you are when orienteering. What are these?
13. In your opinion, what abilities does orienteering test?
14. Explain what you would do if you got lost when orienteering.
15. Name and draw a map of your orienteering region, showing where local club(s) are based and the location and names of known woods/forests used for events.
16. List the things which orienteering maps show but which are *not* shown on OS maps.
17. Copy the following timescale and briefly state the significance of each year to the sport of orienteering.

    1890 (W)   1966 (W)
    1918 (W)   1967 (B)
    1946 (W)   1976 (B)
    1962 (B)   1979 (W)
    1965 (B)   1985 (W)
    B = British significance;
    W = World significance

The next three questions are to be answered together in the form of an essay, so that question 18 is the introduction, 19 the main part and 20 the conclusion.

Title: **The Sport of Orienteering**

18. Briefly describe what the sport is about and how it has spread throughout the world.
19. Describe simply and clearly what happens at an orienteering event. Include the following:
    1 where to go
    2 what course to choose
    3 how to begin
    4 how to find the way
    5 how to finish
    6 how to find out the results.
20. Explain the sentence: Orienteering is a sport for everyone!

© Ian Lockren 1988   Permission is given to photocopy the above worksheet without fee for use in the institution by which the book is bought.

5 AN INTRODUCTION TO ROCK CLIMBING

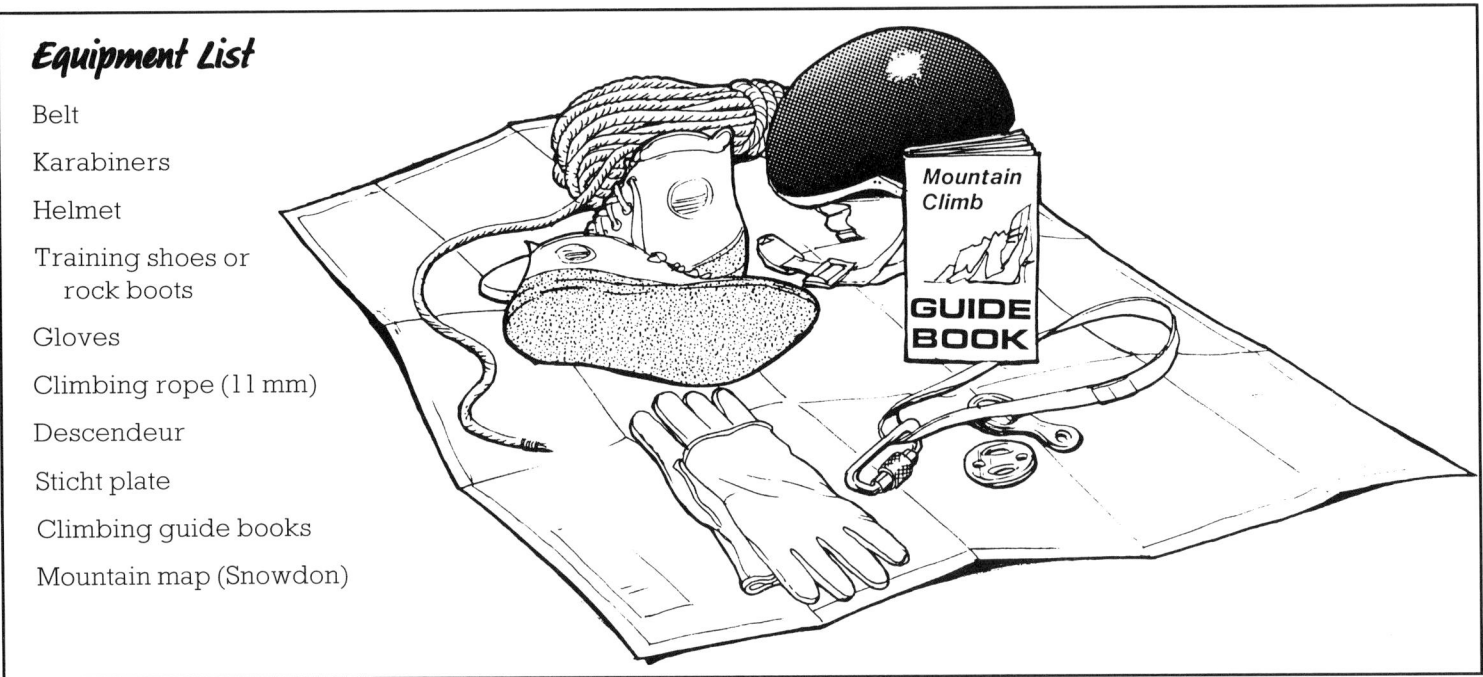

Equipment List

- Belt
- Karabiners
- Helmet
- Training shoes or rock boots
- Gloves
- Climbing rope (11 mm)
- Descendeur
- Sticht plate
- Climbing guide books
- Mountain map (Snowdon)

Introduction

Climbing *rocks*, as distinct from climbing mountains, is a sport in its own right. It grew out of a desire by mountaineers to find and tackle more difficult and challenging routes to the summits of mountains. Now, rock climbers are to be found wherever there are sheer rocks—not just in the mountains, but also in valleys, hills, quarries and on sea cliffs.

Is climbing sheer rocks, sheer madness? Of course, there are dangers in any type of climbing activity, whether you are tackling a roadside boulder or a crag in the Scottish Highlands. However, the risks involved can be reduced to a minimum by learning the correct procedures and using proper safety equipment. These **rock skills** can make rock climbing a safe, exciting and very enjoyable sport. This Chapter extends the discussion on scrambling begun in Chapter 2 (Section 1.4) and provides an introduction to the sport of rock climbing. The first Section looks at the sport in general. Safety procedures and basic skills are developed in the second Section and abseiling is covered in the third Section.

1 ABOUT ROCK CLIMBING

In order to develop a feeling for the sport and an awareness of the all-important safety aspects, it is helpful to consider how, when and why rock climbing arose as a sport in Britain.

Check out your library for books on climbing

1.1 Rock climbing in Britain

Rock climbing has changed a lot since its early days, when it was an activity very closely associated with the related sport of mountaineering. There have been changes in equipment, clothing and technique as the sport has gradually become more specialised and taken on some distinctive characteristics of its own.

How it started

When mountaineering became popular towards the end of the last century, the main idea was to climb to the tops of mountains using the easiest and most accessible routes. This usually meant using **gullies** with plenty of **ledges** which offered safe places to rest. It is best to term this sort of activity **mountain climbing** rather than rock climbing, which, as you will see, has rather different objectives.

The climbing techniques used in these early days were those developed by climbers in the European Alps. For example, ropes were used to tie all the members of the climbing party together. However, the obvious disadvantage of this was that if one member of the group fell, everyone else could follow. Such accidents were often fatal.

Mountain climbing was, initially, an activity enjoyed only by those who had sufficient time and money to be able to travel to places such as the Alps, and relatively few people could afford to do so. The climbers wore caps, heavy tweed suits (with ties) and they usually carried walking sticks. It is interesting to note that the **breeches** worn by the early climbers are similar to those worn by climbers and mountaineers today. (Breeches are trousers which come just below the knee.)

Early climbers in the Alps. Note the clothing. They are crossing the ravine using a stepladder

Much climbing took place in the English Lake District as a form of practice for the European mountains. A small number of climbers made first ascents on more difficult routes here, and it was they who laid the foundations for the newer activity of rock climbing as we know it today.

How it developed

By the 1930s, the Depression in the industrial towns of northern England and central Scotland saw a few working-class people venture into the adjacent mountain areas to lay the basis of a tradition for northern climbing which remains today. During this period the techniques, equipment and style of climbing altered to the extent that the sport could now be truly described as **rock climbing**. The rock climber began to look for harder places to climb. Rather than choosing routes leading up to the mountain tops, the rock climber tackled crags and ascents on the steeper sides of mountains. Interest moved away from the easier gullies to steeper and more exposed **slabs** and **walls**.

As techniques developed, more emphasis was placed on the use of small holds, particularly **footholds**. Climbers began to realise that the rope could offer more in terms of safety. **Belaying** onto rock spikes meant that they could safeguard themselves from falls, and this had the effect of making climbers more willing to try out increasingly difficult routes. Gradually, standards improved and more people became involved in the sport. By the 1950s and 60s, there was intensive development of all the main climbing areas in Britain. Snowdonia took over from the Lake District as the region in which the greatest number of advances in technique and methods were seen. As the improvements in equipment and technique continued, more and more challenging rock features could be tackled (e.g. **steep walls**, **cracks** and **overhangs**) as the climber was given the confidence to improve and experiment.

The **synthetic rope** was becoming universally accepted in place of the traditional kind which was made from natural fibres. Natural fibres had a dangerous tendency to snap if too much weight was put on them. **Belts**, **karabiners** and **chocks** began to be used, and in the 1960s the use of climbing hardware of all kinds 'exploded' with a whole range of protection items and artificial aids, such as **pitons**, **expansion bolts** and **étriers**. A large industry grew to supply the demands for new and improved hardware and mountaineering shops became packed-out with climbing gear, and they remain so today.

As equipment and techniques developed, climbers attempted more difficult routes

Modern climbing

Today, more people than ever are being introduced to the sport. Virtually everyone has access to, or is able to take part in, climbing if they wish. Many schools teach it as part of an outdoor pursuits programme and some even have their own climbing walls.

The sport has developed in three distinct ways.

1 Aid climbing

This is a development which arose from the 1960s explosion of the manufacture of climbing aids or hardware. It involves hammering pitons, pegs or bolts into cracks in the rock. This can, for example, enable climbers to ascend overhangs and routes which would otherwise be impossible.

2 Free climbing

This is the type of climbing with which we are concerned in this Chapter. It involves using a variety of types of safety equipment, (such as ropes) which *protect* the climber from a fall, but which do not assist with the actual climbing itself. You should resist the temptation to 'pull yourself up' using the rope or other pieces of safety equipment.

3 Solo climbing

This involves climbing alone, usually without safety equipment or a rope.

Although most climbers take part in free climbing, there has recently been a growth in unprotected solo climbing. This has developed, it is believed, as a reaction against the over-use of climbing aids and it can be seen as a return to the basic idea of 'climber versus the rock'.

Exercise 1 — Rock climbing in Britain

Briefly describe how each of the following four aspects have developed from the early days of mountain climbing to the modern sport of rock climbing we know today.

1 safety equipment
2 the popularity of the sport
3 the aims of climbing
4 the places where climbing took place

1.2 What is a rock face?

For our purposes, we will define a **rock face** as an outcrop of rock or boulder of any height which requires all four of the climber's limbs to be used in order to climb it.

Whether or not *you* are able to climb it will depend on:
1 its angle of steepness
2 the features on it which can be used for handholds and footholds
3 your experience and ability.

Let's now look at the first two of these points in more detail.

1 Rock steepness

Although the steepness of a rock face usually seems to present most problems for beginners (largely because it can be very off-putting and frightening to have to tackle anything sheer), it does not *always* follow that the steeper the rock is, the more difficult the climb will be. However, more often than not, this is the case.

Special names describe rock faces of different steepness. A rock face with a slope of between 30° and 70° is called a **slab**. This is a fairly easy angle for beginners to climb. There are not usually too many problems resulting from hands and feet slipping off holds.

A **wall** is steeper than a slab. It has a slope of 70° to 90° and generally presents more difficulties for the climber. Where there are plenty of holds available, walls can be

ROCK CLIMBING

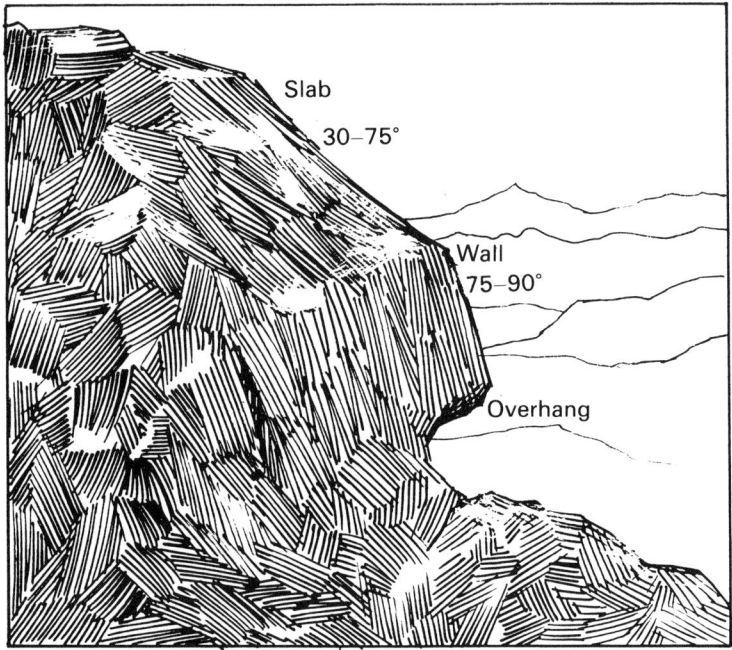

Rock steepness

useful for developing technique and confidence. Indoor climbing walls are also used for this purpose. A wall that projects out is called an **overhang** or **roof** and usually, these can only be climbed after gaining some experience. In many cases, special artificial climbing equipment is necessary.

2 Rock features

You do not need to look too closely at a rock face to see that it is covered with cracks, ledges, bumps and angular edges. These provide the means by which you can make your way up and across the face, from hold to hold, until you reach the top. But holds are not always conveniently placed—you will have to search for them, choose the best ones to use and plan a series of moves from one to another. The holds will also be of different shapes and sizes, some suitable for your whole hand or foot, others only wide enough for fingertips or toes.

Rock faces can show the following features, all of which you are likely to come across sooner or later.

Crack This, as the name suggests, is where the rock is broken into thin and narrow fissures. Some of them will only be wide enough to allow you to fit in fingers or toes, whereas larger cracks allow you to use a fist or foot (this technique is called **jamming**).

Chimney This is the name given to a wide crack, big enough to put your whole body into.

Gully This is wider than a chimney and is usually fairly easy to climb, having plenty of holds and places to stop and rest.

Corner This is the name given to the rock where two walls meet, rather like a corner in a room.

Ledge This is a place where the rock levels off enough to allow you to stand on it with some degree of comfort.

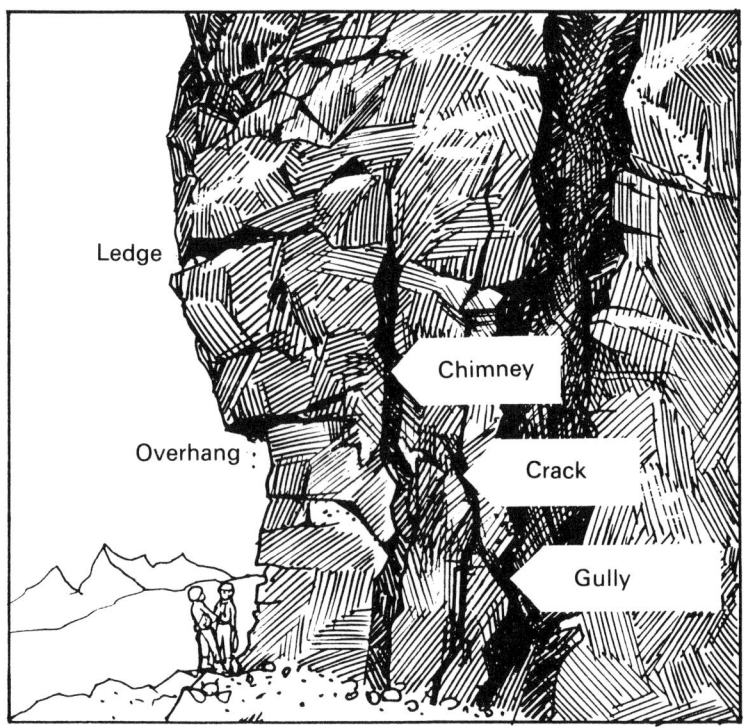

> *Exercise 2*
> Find a local boulder, rock face or climbing wall. Make a sketch of the face and label as many features as you can recognise. A photocopy of your sketch can be used later to plan possible climbing routes.

1.3 How climbs are graded

We already know that the difficulty of a climb will depend partly on the steepness of the rock face and, more importantly, on the availability of holds. An easy climb could be steep but have plenty of large hand and footholds, cracks and ledges. More difficult routes will usually have fewer and smaller rock features, reducing the choice and increasing the skill and experience required.

Climbs in Britain are graded according to their difficulty. The most generally accepted classification system is shown below.

As a beginner you should already be able to climb a route graded M (moderate) and you might well begin with a D route; then, if all goes well, progressing onto a V Diff route. Your rate of progress will be carefully controlled by your instructor/teacher.

Most climbs have names and some of these are quite funny. Wobblestone Crack, for example, a V Diff route on Burbage Edge in the Peak District, is aptly named. If you ever climb this one you will find out why!

In climbing guidebooks you will find the names of individual climbs, their grades, heights and descriptions of routes, as well as information on who made the first ascent and when. Some books even have sketches of rock faces, similar to the one you produced in Exercise 2.

Grade	Abbreviation	Description
Easy	E	A scramble
Moderate	M	Low-angled slab with large holds
Difficult	D (Diff)	Steeper slab
Very difficult	VD (V. diff)	More demanding
Severe	S	Strenuous climbing — experience needed
Very severe	VS	Hard and strenuous
Hard, very severe	HVS	More demanding
Extremely severe	XS	The ultimate test of strength and technique

> *Moorfield's Edge*
> List of climbs.
> 1. *'Blind Alley'* 15.25 m/50 feet VD
> A deep gulley is taken until it is possible to climb the slab, which is divided into two ledges. Mantleshelf the ledges then climb the final steeper wall via the thin crack, avoiding the overhang on the right.
> 2. *'Left Eye Chimney'* 12 m/40 feet D
> Start on the right of the slab. Traverse onto it, then continue direct.

Guide books are a must: they contain much useful information on route difficulty, etc.

ROCK CLIMBING

> *Exercise 3*
> Obtain a copy of a climbing guidebook. Try to get one which shows a nearby area or a place which you will visit in the future. (Guidebooks are available from mountain shops or bookshops. See also the addresses given at the end of this Chapter). Once you have your book:
> 1. Find out the rock type and how this might affect climbing.
> 2. Comment on the variety of routes available, particularly those of your own standard (D, V Diff).
> 3. Choose a route that appeals to you, draw a sketch of it and add the information given in the guidebook's text to your drawing.

1.4 Where to climb

You should be able to gain some climbing experience no matter where you live. The exact nature of this experience will depend on what facilities are available locally or within reasonable travelling distance. Indoor climbing walls are excellent for both beginners, who require a safe and controlled environment in which to learn and develop good basic habits, and for experienced climbers wanting to practise certain aspects of their technique or simply to keep 'in trim' during the winter.

It is important that you approach climbing walls in the right frame of mind. The aim is not to 'conquer' the wall itself, because in many cases, the relative ease with which this can be done can produce dangerous overconfidence. Climbing walls are used to train for the 'real' rock, so always remember that outdoor conditions may make the climbing more difficult. No matter how good the indoor facilities are, sooner or later you will want to feel and experience a real rock face. The simplest and probably most easily available is the boulder or roadside rock outcrop. 'Bouldering' is an acceptable way of learning climbing skills and even a small outcrop of rock can produce a number of challenging problems.

Climbing walls are excellent for safe practice

> *Exercise 4*
> Find out **(1)** what local climbing facilities exist (indoor climbing walls, boulders and outcrops), and **(2)** where people from your area go to climb.

2 BEGINNING CLIMBING

In this Section you will learn the basics of how to climb. This includes an understanding of the simple safety procedures, developing the techniques to get you off the ground and gaining experience using different kinds of specialist equipment. The most important aspect, though, and the key to enjoyment and possible future participation at any level, is to aquire *good safety habits*. Let's look first at the equipment that will help you to develop good safety habits.

2.1 Basic equipment

For personal clothing, Chapter 2 Section 1.5 should be your guide. You need inner clothes to keep you warm and an outer shell to help you stay dry. Your clothing should certainly include gloves. You will want them not only to stop your hands from getting cold while waiting for your turn to climb, but also to protect your skin from being injured by the ropes.

Specialist climbing equipment is constantly being tested by the British Mountaineering Council (BMC) and the Union Internationale des Associations d'Alpinisme (UIAA—an international body with representatives from the various countries which have mountaineering clubs), to make sure it is safe to use. To begin with, you must have access to, and knowledge of, the following:
1 rope
2 belt
3 helmet
4 footwear

1 Rope

This is the most important item of safety equipment. Quite literally, your life could depend on your rope, and because of this, climbing ropes are probably the most tested and improved items of equipment.

Climbing ropes are designed to absorb the energy of a falling body in a gradual way so that the climber is cushioned from the full effects of the fall. In order to do this, the rope must be able to *stretch*, but it must not stretch so much that it breaks! An indication of the strength of a rope is given by its breaking strain.

Basic climbing equipment

Type of rope	Size/mm	Number	Approx. breaking strain/kg
Hawser-laid	5	1	450
	7	2	900
	10	3	1500
	11	4	1900
Kernmantel	9	—	1450
	11	4	2250

ROCK CLIMBING

Modern climbing ropes are manufactured from nylon fibres but it must *not* be assumed that all nylon ropes are suitable for climbing use. Many modern sailing ropes are made of nylon but they should never be used for climbing. The only way to be sure if you have a recommended rope is to look for the 'UIAA approved' symbol.

However, synthetic ropes do have some disadvantages. The main one is that because they are made of soft material, they can be damaged by sharp stones and edges. Also, the material has a low melting point, therefore you should be careful not to allow one rope to run over another, because the heat generated by friction could cause the ropes to melt and weaken. Check for signs of wear.

There are two types of synthetic ropes available:

(a) Hawser-laid As can be seen below, this type consists of three strands of nylon twisted together. Size 4 (11 mm) is recommended for climbing. Although this is the cheaper of the two types of synthetic rope, the most popular is the Kernmantel.

(b) Kernmantel This type consists of an inner core of long nylon strands bunched inside a braided and colourful outer covering. The rope is smoother than Hawser-laid, so it feels nicer and gives less friction. Also, it does not kink as much. It is usual to climb with 45 m of 11 mm rope, although the use of *two* 9 mm ropes has become popular with experienced climbers.

Rope skills are used a great deal and it is important to know how to handle and care for a rope even before making your first visit to a rock face. Coiling a rope after use is the best way of carrying and storing it. Correct coiling also ensures that the rope will uncoil safely, thereby reducing the chances of the rope becoming tangled, which wastes time and could be dangerous.

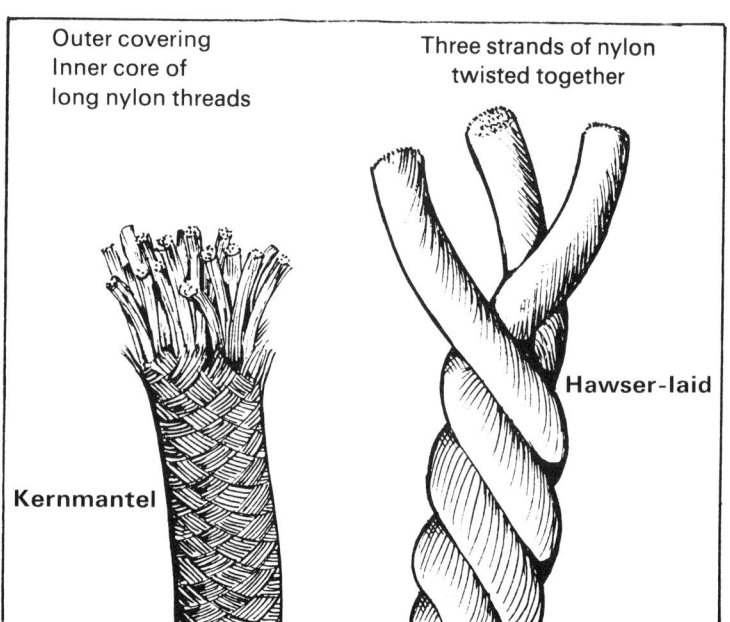

Exercise 5—Coiling and uncoiling

1. To tie-off a coil:
    (i) Take a rope that has been coiled and tied-off.
    (ii) Unfasten the tie-off.
    (iii) Re-fasten the rope by forming a loop with one end of the rope and then winding the other end around both the loop and coils. Make more than three winds, but not more than six. Then place the end through the loop and pull the tie-off tight.
2. To uncoil a rope:
    (i) Unfasten the tie-off.
    (ii) Release a coil at a time, letting them fall to the ground one on top of the other so that the rope does not tangle.
3. To coil a rope:
    (i) Take the rope in one hand about half a metre from the end.
    (ii) Simply coil it over your hand, making sure that the coils are of equal lengths and that they lie flat.
    (iii) When you have about a metre left, find the beginning of the rope, form a loop and tie-off as before.

CLIMBING EQUIPMENT

1 **2**

Tying off a coil. Make sure the coils are of equal length and that they lie flat

3

4

2 Waistbelt and karabiner

The simplest and original method of attaching a rope to a climber was to tie the end around the climber's waist. However this is not particularly comfortable and has in the past lead to suffocation when climbers have been left hanging after a fall for even a short time. Therefore, today, it is usual to use a special **waistbelt**, which helps to spread the load, or a **harness**, which gives even more comfort by taking the weight under the thighs as well.

The most popular belt is the **troll**, which is shown on the right. This is made from nylon webbing and has a separate ring on which a karabiner can be clipped. The combined breaking strain is 2000 kg.

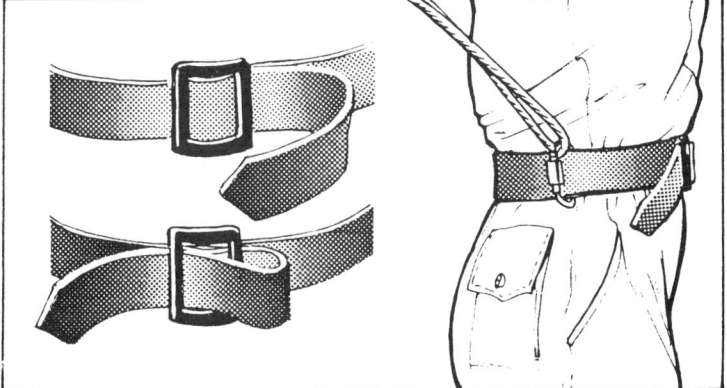

Get into the habit of double-buckling belts

ROCK CLIMBING

A karabiner (or 'krab' for short) is the name given to the metal link. It has a spring loaded **gate** which opens so that a rope can be inserted and attached to the belt. The gate closes with a reasuring 'click' and can be made secure by screwing-up the screw-gate.

Krabs are vital 'links' to safe climbing, so it is important to treat them carefully. Keep them clean and don't drop them—metal can crack inside without you even knowing there is anything wrong until it's too late.

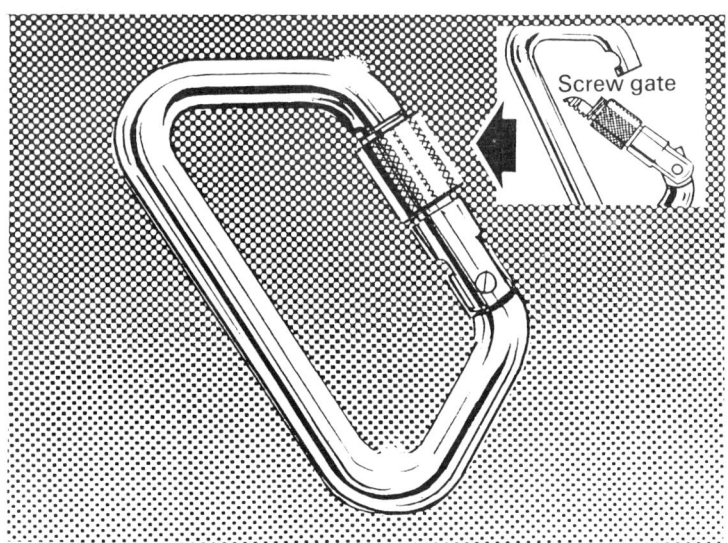

Exercise 6—Wearing a belt

You will notice that the belt on page 91 has been **double buckled**. This means that the tail of the belt has been threaded back through the buckle to give added safety.

Select a belt that fits (small, medium or large), put it on and do it up in the normal way—once through the buckle. Then pull. You will see how easily the tail slides and the belt unbuckles. Now double buckle the belt. The difference is frightening!

3 Helmet

Helmets have become accepted wear by climbers of all abilities. It is strongly recommended that you get into the habit of *always* using one, whether climbing or merely waiting on the ground for your turn. You should certainly wear one when climbing above the level of your own height. Helmets provide protection from falling equipment or rocks and help prevent head injuries in the event of a climber falling. The Mountain Rescue Committee state that because more climbers are now using helmets, there has been a reduction in the number of head injuries.

Modern helmets are light, made from fibreglass and weigh 680–770 g. They are well padded inside and have fully adjustable chin and head straps. Not all helmets have UIAA approval but it is best to choose one that does.

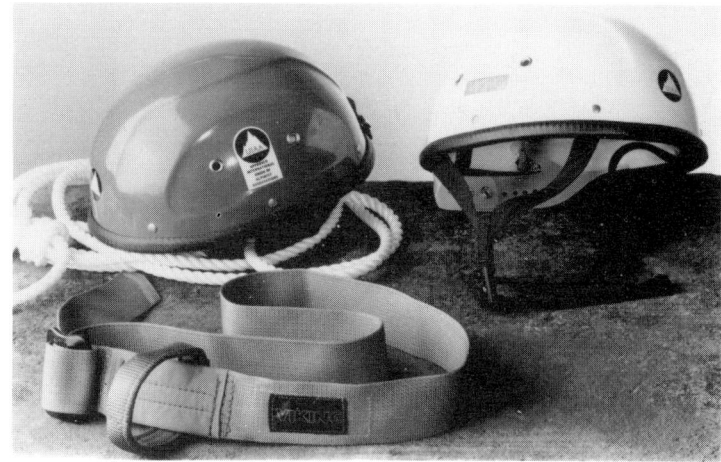

It is advisable to use approved and tested equipment. Look out for the UIAA mark

CLIMBING SKILLS

4 Footwear

Mountain-walking boots are the normal type of footwear used for climbing, particularly by beginners. The rigid soles on walking boots protect the feet and help with footholds. However, when working indoors or on a low crag or boulder, pumps or training shoes are ideal. They offer more freedom of movement and flexibility, which can often be useful.

Experienced climbers usually own a pair of special, lightweight rock climbing boots. These strange-looking articles were originally developed by Pierre Allain in the 1950s and were called after him ('PAs') although more common today are the similar-looking 'EBs'. These lightweight boots have smooth rubber soles which give very effective friction grips, even on the smallest of footholds.

Rock boots

We have now considered the basic equipment you will need to start climbing on an indoor wall, boulder or low crag. But before taking a step off the ground, it is vital that you understand some important safety procedures.

2.2 Safety first

Our aim now is to begin developing good climbing habits in a carefully-controlled way, at all times under the direction of a teacher/instructor. We shall start by looking at **bouldering**, the use of a **top rope** and the various **climbing calls** which contribute to safety and enjoyment.

Bouldering

You can gain experience at climbing boulders, low crags or climbing walls without having to use a rope, belt, etc. Under the supervision of your teacher/instructor, you should work at a low height—usually no more than twice your own height. Boulders can be used in a number of ways to develop confidence as much as climbing skill.

> *Exercise 7—Bouldering*
> 1 As directed by your teacher/instructor, get plenty of practice moving up (no more than twice your height) traversing (going across) and descending (never jump down) boulders.
> 2 Follow the leader in a traverse. Do what your teacher/instructor does and you will find that it is possible to come across quite difficult climbing problems and yet be near to the ground at all times.

A challenging climbing wall

Top rope belaying

When learning to climb on an indoor wall, boulder or low crag, your teacher/instructor will probably use a **top rope belay system**. This is very safe and works in the following way.

The safety rope is clipped into the krab of the climber's belt and runs up to the top of the climb, through another krab that is attached to something secure, and then back down to the teacher/instructor who is standing next to the climber. As the climber moves up, the instructor will continually take the rope in, to keep it fairly tight. This will safeguard the climber from a fall to the ground. The instructor is **belaying** (the name given to the technique used for taking-in the safety rope). The instructor can also be described as the **belayer**.

Climbing calls

Before you start to climb, the belayer will check the climbing equipment, the helmet and that the belt is double-buckled, the rope is on and the krab is screwed-up. Then, when you are in position and the belayer is ready, he/she will say: 'Climb when ready'.

When you are ready, you reply: 'Climbing'. However, do not actually start climbing until you have been given the go-ahead by the belayer, who says: 'Okay'.

These climbing calls should be used all the time. Later on, you will learn other calls to use in different situations.

> *Exercise 8—Top rope climbing*
> Your teacher will arrange a top rope belay for you. Take it in turns to climb no higher than about 4 metres from the ground. Climbing style is not important at this stage, but getting used to the belaying, the equipment and the climbing calls, is. Once you have reached the given height or choose not to go any further, simply climb back down and the rope will be let out for you by the belayer.
> The importance of careful down-climbing cannot be overstressed. It is more difficult because you cannot see the holds so easily, but it is a technique you must be at ease with if you want to be able to lead climbs.

Belaying

2.3 Holding on and moving up

Once you are sure about the safety procedures relating to belaying, climbing calls and equipment, it is time to look more closely at how to climb.

Try to imagine how you would climb on all fours up the stairs at home. You would probably move first a hand, then a foot, followed by the other hand and then the other foot, and so on up. This is also the way you should move up a climbing wall or rock face. The idea is to move *one* limb at a time so that you always have the other three (two feet and one hand or two hands and one foot) in contact with the rock or wall surface.

Having left the ground, you are likely to make two main mistakes:

1 Over-use of hands. Most people tend to rely on handholds far too much, which results in 'hanging' by the arms and overreaching. Instead try to make as much use as possible of your legs. Your leg muscles are bigger and stronger and more used to supporting your weight than your arms. Try to select holds which are big enough to stand on and push-off from. Your hands should only really be used for balance; they should be kept low, at about shoulder level, to allow you to go from foothold to foothold. This does take practice, but the sooner you are able to let your legs do most of the work, the sooner you will find that climbing will become less tiring, less of a scramble and more enjoyable.

2 Hugging the rock. A very common mistake is to lean into the rock because this feels safer. Instead, you should try to lean *out* so that you can (a) see what you are doing; and, at the same time, (b) keep your feet pressed into the rock, rather than away from it.

Practise climbing using the hints suggested above. If you get stuck, never be afraid to go back a few holds to a resting place and work out another route. Try to think in terms of a *series* of moves, rather than single ones.

Points to remember:
1 Think *footholds, footholds*!
2 Always have three limbs in contact with the climbing surface.
3 Don't hug the rock.
4 Work out a series of moves to go from one resting hold to another. In other words: plan ahead.

Exercise 9—Good style
Experiment using these four approaches.
1 Climb using your *hands* as much as possible—reaching high for holds and pulling yourself up.
2 Lean *into* the wall or rock.
Now try:
3 Climbing using your *feet* and keeping your arms *low*.
4 Leaning *out* as much as you dare do.

Rock provides us with a variety of bumps, cracks and edges for use as holds. Some of these are small, on which only fingers or edges of boots can be placed. Others are large, allowing you to use the whole of your hand or foot. Larger rock features, such as **ledges**, **cracks** and **chimneys** require the use of particular climbing techniques.

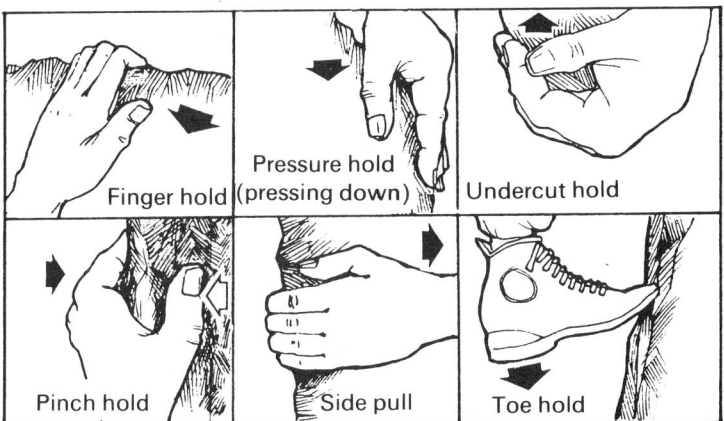

Finger hold | Pressure hold (pressing down) | Undercut hold
Pinch hold | Side pull | Toe hold

ROCK CLIMBING

Climbing onto a ledge

This technique is called **mantelshelfing**. It consists of four basic movements, as shown below. The same method is used to climb out of the deep end of a swimming pool.

When mantelshelfing, try to get your foot (not your knee) onto the ledge

Climbing cracks

Cracks vary in width, but narrow ones can be climbed by jamming fingers, hands, arms, legs or feet into the crack. **Hand and foot jamming** is the most useful method. The idea is to ease your hand in then lock it in place, so that it can be used as a support. With a foot jam, you twist your boot sideways, put it in, then straighten it again. Reverse the sequence to remove your foot. Where there is enough rock on one side of a crack to place your feet, a technique called the **layback** can be used.

The layback works using the pull of the hands around the edge of the crack and the push of the feet on the wall surface. You then just walk up the rock face, leaning back on your hands and moving up on your feet. It is important not to allow hands to get too far ahead of feet—the steeper the rock, the closer hands and feet need to be.

Hand jamming can be rather painful!

CLIMBING SKILLS

Layback

Climbing chimneys

The best way to tackle a chimney is to push against both walls. There are two ways of doing this. **Bridging** involves placing one hand and foot on each wall, using the available holds and climbing up in the normal way. **Backing** involves placing both hands on one wall and both feet on the other.

> *Exercise 10*
> Locate and climb the following rockface features:
>   Ledge (mantelshelfing)
>   Cracks (jamming and layback)
>   Chimney (bridging and backing)

Bridging

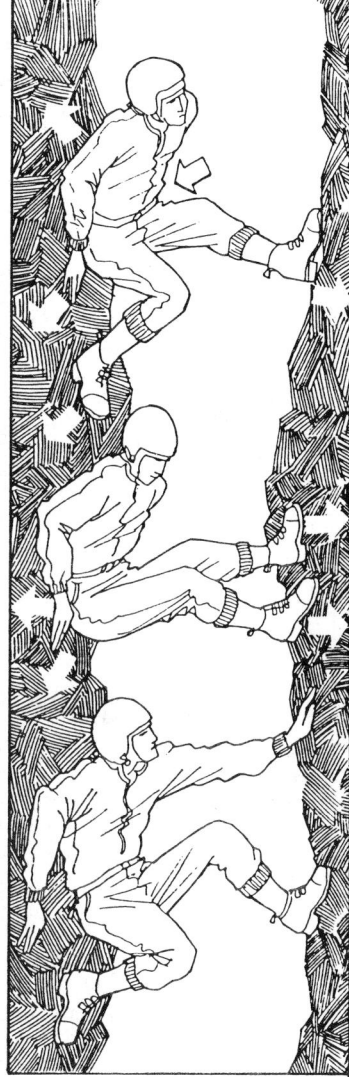
Backing—usually easier

2.4 Knots

So far, all your safety knots will have been tied for you. Now it is time to learn to tie yourself on to a belay rope. However, always check with your teacher/instructor that you have tied the knot correctly before climbing.

All knots reduce the strength of a climbing rope. Therefore, it is important that the knots themselves are as strong and resistant to slipping as possible. A variety of knots can be used, but the most useful is the **figure-of-eight knot**. Its main advantages are as follows:

1. It is easy to tie.
2. It can be used in most climbing situations.
3. It is fairly easy to unfasten after use.
4. If tied incorrectly, it still results in a reasonably safe overhand knot.

Exercise 11—Learning to tie a figure-of-eight knot

1. To attach the rope to your waistbelt krab, take a loop of about 30 cm and follow the procedure shown below. Compare your knot with your friends'. Is it an '8' shape? If it isn't, then it is probably an overhand knot. To be able to tie a figure-of-eight knot properly takes some practice.

2. This time, imagine there is something wrong with your belt and you cannot use it. You need to tie directly onto the rope, so you must tie a loop large enough to step into and tighten at your waist. Practise this to try to get the correct size.

3. Next try this: Take the end of the rope, tie a single figure-of-eight knot and pass the end of the rope around your waist or other suitable object. Then thread the rope through the knot, as shown below, but make sure that the threaded-back rope is on the *inside* of the knot.

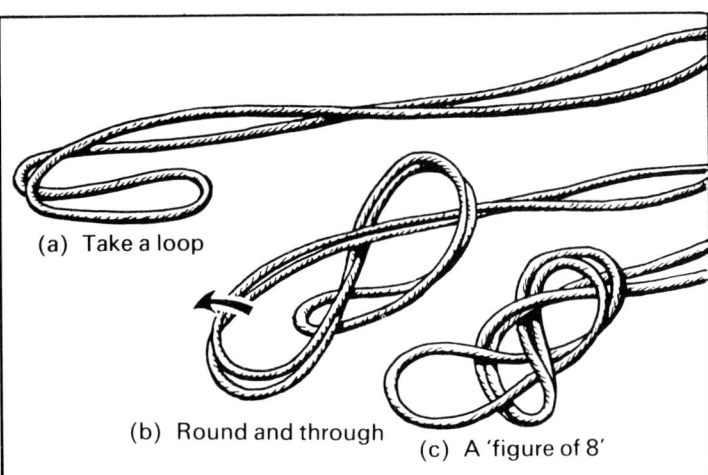

(a) Take a loop
(b) Round and through
(c) A 'figure of 8'

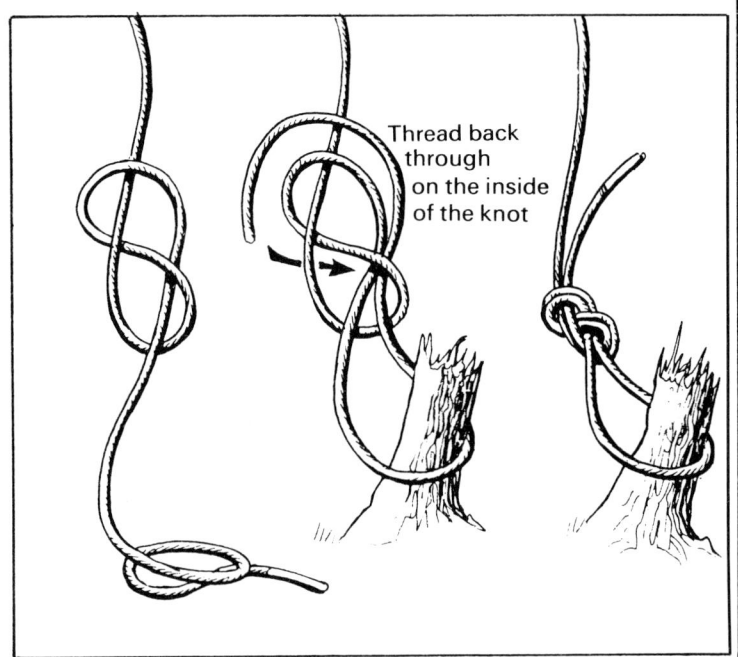

Thread back through on the inside of the knot

2.5 Learning to belay

The key to safe climbing is safe belaying. Therefore it needs to be stressed that here, as in every aspect of climbing, you should never attempt anything which you are not capable of tackling safely. Your teacher/instructor will not put you in a position where you are responsible for belaying others until you are ready and experienced enough to cope with this very important technique. As a safe form of practice, you can belay on the flat, using the **hip belay** technique or the **Sticht plate** technique. However, even when you can perform both of these adequately, you may still not be ready to belay on a rock face.

Exercise 12—Hip belaying
Your teacher/instructor will arrange a practice session which will involve taking-in the rope around your waist or through the wall bars in a gym, but without a climber on the other end.
Take the 'live rope' (i.e. the rope between you and the imaginary climber) in your right hand. Pass the rope around your back under your left arm (not over it) and once around the wrist and into your left hand. The rope leaving your left hand is called the 'dead rope' and it should ideally drop in a neat coil on the ground.
You are now in the 'Get set' position as shown below. Follow the sequence through to the 'Pull' stage. You should *never let go of the rope* at any stage. When belaying for real, leather gloves should be worn and they should protect the wrist area as well as the hands.

Exercise 13—Sticht plate belaying
The Sticht plate was developed by Fritz Sticht to simplify the technique of belaying and has largely replaced the 'round the back' method, described previously.
A practice session will be set up for you. Instead of pulling the rope around your waist and twisting it over the left hand for friction, you simply push a loop through the plate, clip it into the waist krab and feed it through from right hand into left as the climber moves up. If a fall occurs, the idea is to pull the rope into the body so that the plate is pressed into the krab, producing a braking effect.

Exercise 14—Belaying on the flat
Take it in turns to be the belayer and the climber on flat ground. Pass the rope through a suitable holder—low wall bars in a gym or the base of an upturned bench will do. As one of you attaches to the rope and walks forward, the other belays.

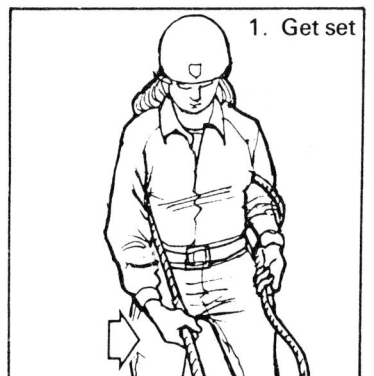
1. Get set

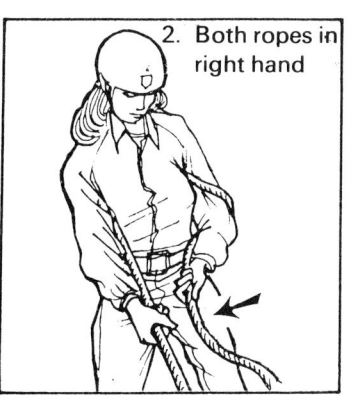
2. Both ropes in right hand

3. Slide up

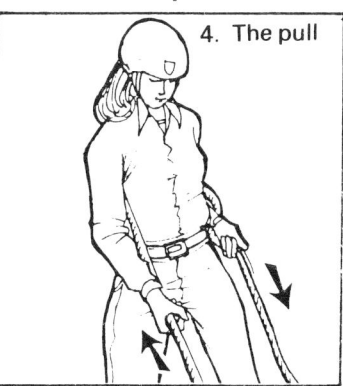
4. The pull

ROCK CLIMBING

> *Exercise 15—Holding a fall*
> Set up the top rope belay as if for climbing. Using a heavy weight, such as a rugby tackling bag, take it in turns to feel what it would be like to have to hold someone who has fallen. The idea is to *gradually* hold the fall rather than stopping it suddenly—which would be difficult and could injure your back. You do this by bringing both arms into your body. The friction on the rope should be enough to arrest the fall.

3 ABSEILING

This Section completes your introduction to rock climbing by looking at the technique called **abseiling**.

Abseiling (pronounced 'ab-sile-ing'), a German word, is the name given to a controlled slide down a rope. It is a very useful technique to learn, enabling you to get down from the top of a climb, as well as being a very enjoyable activity in its own right. However, it can also be one of the most dangerous procedures, relying purely on the strength of anchor points and the rope. It is important, therefore, that all the safety guidelines are followed, and this should always include the use of separate **safety rope**.

There are a number of different ways of abseiling but the two most acceptable methods are:

1 The **classic abseil**—the original method using no equipment other than the rope itself, which is passed around the body. This provides the friction to control the descent.
2 **Abseiling using a descendeur**—there are various metal devices available which are designed to make abseiling quicker and more comfortable. Probably the safest and easiest to use is the **figure-of-eight descendeur**.

A 'figure-of-eight' abseil

Clip into waist krab

ABSEILING

Exercise 16—A 'classic' experience

The only real advantage of the classic method of abseiling is that it does not require any specialist equipment. For this reason alone, it should be practised because it could be useful in an emergency. Your instructor will probably want to introduce this on the flat, by attaching a rope to a suitable anchor point, as follows.

(i) Place the rope on the ground and stand over it—one foot each side—facing the anchor.
(ii) Take the rope from behind you up across your chest and over your left shoulder and into your right hand.
(iii) With your left hand holding the rope in front, walk backwards feeding the rope through with your right (controlling) hand.

The next step is to try this out on a rock face. Your teacher/instructor will make sure that you have a totally separate safety rope attached to your belt which will be belayed in the normal way.

Exercise 17—How to use a descendeur

Your instructor will prepare the ropes so that you can:

(i) practise feeding a double rope through a figure-of-eight descendeur as illustrated on page 100.
(ii) turn your waistbelt into a **sit harness** for comfort. For this, you will be provided with a **sling**—if it's a short one, put it on as shown below, or, if it is rather long, try the 'nappie' method.

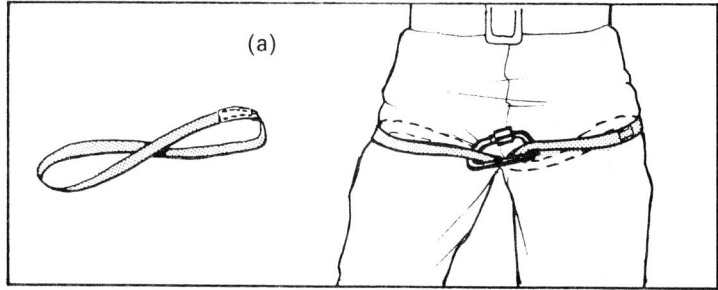

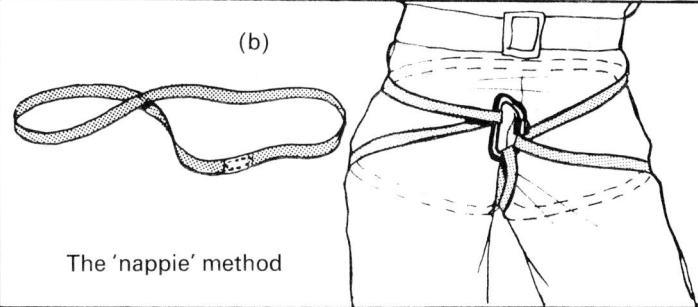

The 'nappie' method

(iii) practise an abseil on the flat or down a grass bank. After your teacher/instructor has set-up the rope, push a loop of it through the descendeur and attach it to your right-hand side (or the other side if you are left-handed). Walk backwards, feeding the rope through the descendeur with your controlling hand. The other hand can grip the rope between you and the anchor to provide balance.

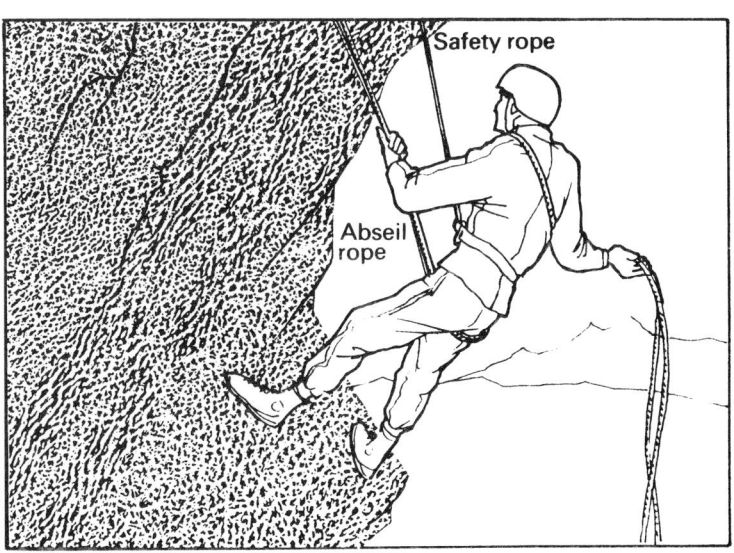

Preparing to abseil

A suitable place from which to abseil should have at least two good anchor points, and be set up in the following way.

1. *The abseil rope.* This is usually doubled so that the middle can be looped over a spike, or a figure-of-eight knot tied and clipped into a krab. The rest of the rope will then be thrown down to the ground—and a check made to see that it reaches the bottom!
2. *The safety rope.* This will be set-up in a fashion similar to that used for normal belaying. The only difference here is that the rope is going to be clipped onto someone who is already at the top and is abseiling *down*, instead of someone being at the bottom, climbing up. It is important that the safety rope is kept completely separate from the abseil rope. It is attached to the waistbelt at the side by another krab.

Safe abseiling

Abseiling from a rock face

Here is the check list of safety points and techniques.
1. Always use a safety rope on a separate krab.
2. Wear gloves to belay and abseil.
3. Use a sit sling 'nappie'.
4. Begin abseiling by walking backwards down the rock, letting out the rope with your controlling hand as you go.
5. Lean back, keeping your body low and feet high.
6. Don't 'bounce' down, it may put too much strain on the anchors.

Conclusion

In this Chapter we have covered some of the basic safety aspects and techniques of rock climbing. At every stage, your teacher/instructor will have stressed the dangers of overconfidence and your progress will have been strictly matched with your knowledge and ability. If you enjoyed the work you may well wish to learn more, to be able to set up your own belays, tackle single then multi-pitch routes and get to use more advanced techniques and items of equipment. This could eventually take you on to leading a climb yourself. The National Outdoor Training Centres and the BMC run climbing courses. The addresses to write to are given in the Further Information section which follows. But no matter at what level you climb, the same basic rule applies: *safe climbing depends upon developing good climbing habits*. There are no short cuts to experience, so climb safely and enjoy it!

FURTHER INFORMATION

Governing bodies/organisations

British Mountaineering Council (BMC)—the governing body for all mountaineering pursuits, including rock climbing. The Council provides a great deal of valuable information. Joining the BMC brings many other advantages, such as subscription to their monthly magazine, High *(which can also be obtained from newsagents). The address can be found at the end of Chapter 2.*

The Mountaineering Council of Scotland— address in Chapter 2.

Magazines

High—*BMC/newsagents*
Climber—*monthly specialist magazine from newsagents or direct from publishers: Holmes McDougall Ltd, Ravenseft House, 302 St. Vincent St., Glasgow G2 5NL.*
The Great Outdoors—*this general mountaineering magazine often has articles of interest to the rock climber, although it is principally aimed at hill walkers. Available from newsagents or direct from Holmes McDougall (address above).*

Guidebooks

Every mountain area in Britain (and some coastal cliffs and quarries) have special guidebooks written about them, for the rock climber. The BMC also publish guidebooks and they will advise on which ones cover your area of interest.

Other books can be bought from book and mountain shops, or direct from the publisher. For example: Cicernone Press produce a variety of guidebooks, from scrambles to rock climbs, and cover modern techniques. The address is: Cicernone Press, Harmony Hall, Milnthorpe, Cumbria LA7 7QE.

Constable publish a selection of very good general guidebooks covering The Lake District, Wales, Scotland and The Peak District. The address is: Constable & Co. Ltd, 10 Orange St, London WC2H 7EG.

National outdoor training centres

England and Wales: Plas-y-Brenin, Capel Curig, Gwynedd, North Wales, LL24 0ET.
Scotland: Glenmore Lodge, Aviemore, Inverness-shire, PH22 1QU.

WORKSHEET

1. What do the letters UIAA and BMC stand for?

2. What is described as 'a climbers most vital piece of equipment'?

3. Write down the three basic climbing calls used by the belayer and the climber so that the table is completed.

Call	Said by	Action taken
1		
2		
3		

4. What is a belay?

5. Explain what a 'top rope system' of belaying means.

6. What is abseiling?

7. Describe, as if explaining to a beginner, how to wear a waistbelt and how to convert this into a 'nappie' for abseiling.

8. Describe, using a diagram, how a figure-of-eight descendeur works.

9. List the climbing grades that you know in order of difficulty.

10. What do you think is the difference between a single and a multi-pitch climb?

11. Draw and label a karabiner.

12. What are the advantages of synthetic rope over natural fibre?

13. Why are kernmantel ropes often preferred to Hawser-laid?

14. A safety rope should always be used when abseiling but it should be kept separate from the abseil rope. Why?

15. Briefly describe each of the following rock face features:
    (a) crack
    (b) chimney
    (c) gully
    (d) corner
    (e) ledge

16. Select one of the features from question 15 and explain the techniques used to climb it.

17. Describe, with the use of a diagram, how to belay using either:
    (a) waist belay, or
    (b) Sticht plate.

© Ian Lockren 1988 Permission is given to photocopy the above worksheet without fee for use in the institution by which the book is bought.

WORKSHEET

The next three questions are to be answered together in the form of a short essay, with Question 18 as the introduction, 19 the main part and 20 forming the conclusion.

Title: **The Development of British Rock Climbing**

18 What is the difference between mountaineering and rock climbing, and when did the latter start to become a sport in its own right?

19 Rock climbing has changed quite a lot since the early days of the sport. Explain this statement by describing:
   (a) the sort of people who climbed then and who climb now
   (b) the sort of equipment used then and now
   (c) the general standard of climbing then and now.

20 At one time, climbing was restricted to a very few people who had the time and money to spare. Today, it is available to all. In what ways has climbing become a nationwide sport?

© Ian Lockren 1988   Permission is given to photocopy the above worksheet without fee for use in the institution by which the book is bought.

6 CANOEING

Equipment List

Canoe (kayak)

Paddle

Life jacket/buoyancy aid

Helmet

Spray cover

Mountain map

Local map

Books: *Guide to the Waterways of the British Isles* (British Canoe Union publication)

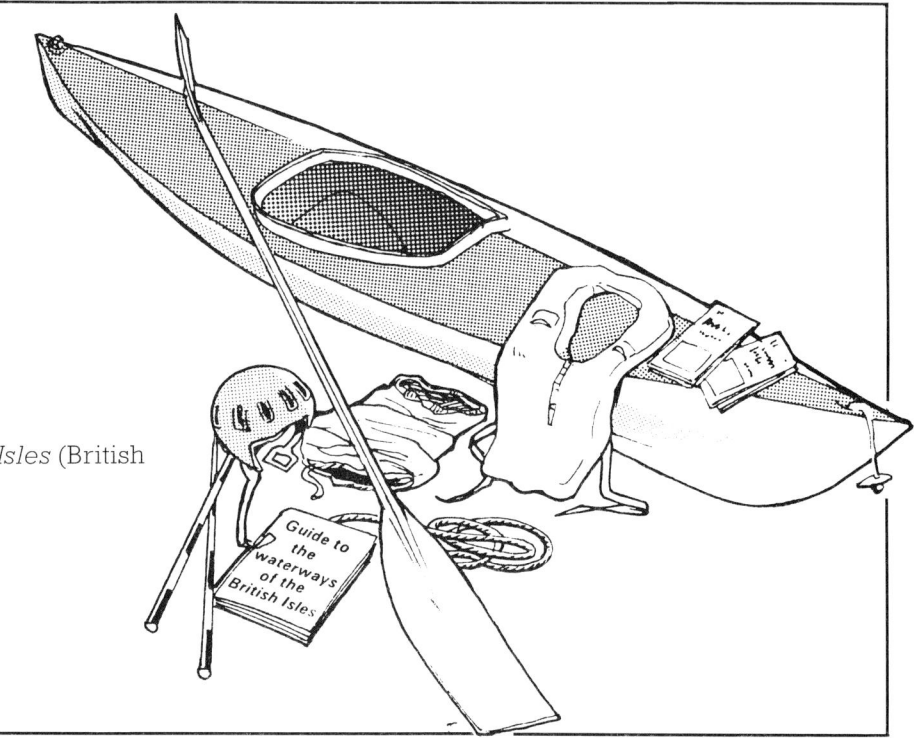

Introduction

For anyone intending to take up the pursuit of canoeing, there is one important and obvious pre-condition: the ability to swim. If you can't swim, then you shouldn't canoe. Learn to swim instead and come back to canoeing once you are confident in the water. From the outset, you need to accept that you will often find yourself in the water, so it's important that this should not frighten you.

This Chapter is divided into three Sections. The first of these will give you the necessary background information about the many aspects of canoeing, how they developed, the kinds of boats used, and the problems associated with getting onto the water.

In Section 2, you will learn how to develop confidence and gain experience in the basic safety, paddling and water skills which are designed to take you to placid (still) water rivers, lakes and canals.

The third Section extends this knowledge and skill to include deeper water. By then, you should have the necessary skills to take-up the sport in one form or another. You may, for example, want to join a club or become a member of your National Association in order to gain further experience and enjoy paddling in the future.

1 ABOUT CANOEING

The general term *canoeing* is used to describe a whole collection of sports and activities which involve canoes. For example, canoes are used:
1. on inland water (rivers, lakes and canals) for racing, e.g. sprint, wild water, slalom and long distance marathon racing, as well as the recreational pursuits of touring and canoe camping.
2. on the sea, for canoe surfing, sailing and long distance trips.
3. in the swimming pool, for the game of canoe polo, in addition to training and skills development.

The sports and water conditions required vary considerably in each case. Slalom canoeing on a fast moving river, for instance, is very different from sprinting on a lake. The first requires a canoe which allows quick turns and manoeuvres to be made; in the second, the main objective is high speed in a straight line. Such differences between water conditions and the uses to which the canoe is put have resulted in a vast range of different designs of craft. You will discover some of these as you work through this Section. First, however, it is interesting to find out how canoeing started and developed into the world-wide sport it is today.

> *Exercise 1 — The sports of canoeing*
> Add as many 'paddles' as you can to the following diagram to illustrate the diversity of the activities that make use of canoes.

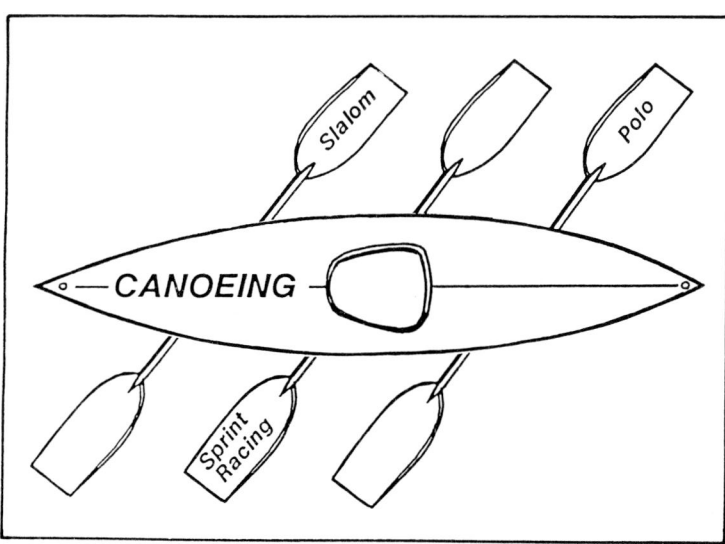

CANOEING

1.1 The history of canoeing

We will look at the history of the sport in three stages:
1. How it began
2. How it developed
3. The state of the sport today

How it began

Modern canoeing owes its existence to the traditions practised by two peoples in their everyday lives.

1. The Eskimos of Greenland developed the **kayak** canoe for use on long sea hunting trips. Their need was for comfort, warmth and dryness and a low position on the water in order to reduce wind resistance. Therefore the Eskimo canoe has a covered deck and the canoeist sits down in the canoe and uses a double-ended paddle.
2. The Red Indian used what is known as the **Canadian** canoe for hunting and travelling on the rivers of North America. A single blade paddle was used and the canoeist knelt rather than sat, so that he or she was high enough to see river rapids or animals to hunt. The Canadian canoe was wide, very stable and open-decked.

Today the differences between these two basic types of canoe can be summarised as shown in the following table.

	Canadian	**Kayak**
Position of canoeist	Half-kneeling	Sitting
Type of paddle	Single blade	Double blade
Deck	Open	Closed

Note, however, that Canadian canoes sometimes now have closed decks to prevent water entering when these boats are used for white water competition.

Abbreviations are often used for the two types of canoe (K for kayak and C for Canadian), so that a one person canoe would be K1 or C1 and a two person, K2 or C2.

The rest of this Chapter is concerned with kayak rather than Canadian canoes, but some of the general information and water skills can be applied to both. We concentrate on kayaks because your first experiences with canoes are likely to involve this type, particularly if you learn in a

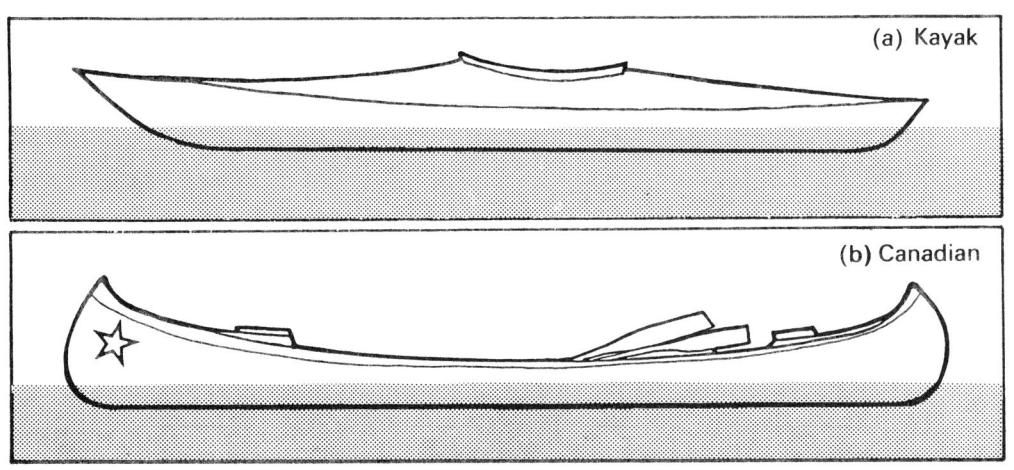
(a) Kayak
(b) Canadian

swimming pool. The Canadian canoe is not nearly as widespread in this country, however it is becoming more popular, and if you do get a chance to use one, you may well prefer it—many do. From now on, though, whenever canoe is mentioned in this book, think kayak!

How it developed

Canoes have been used for hundreds of years to assist Eskimos and Indians with hunting and as important forms of transport, but it was not until the middle of the last century that canoeing developed as a recreational activity and sport. In Britain races were organised on the River Thames and wooden kayaks were used. These were not easily transported and so were kept close to the river. Because the sport was restricted to only a small proportion of the population (the wealthy) it did not really 'take-off' and, in fact, declined a little until the early part of this century.

In the 1920s canoeing received a boost when a German called Hans Klepper developed the **folding kayak**. This craft consisted of a wooden frame covered in canvas which could be folded-up, and was a great advance in design because it allowed people to travel to more distant water, taking their canoes with them. Previously, they had only been able to canoe where there was a club. The folding canoe came to Britain in the 1930s and had an immediate effect on the numbers of people taking up the sport. In 1936, all the canoeing clubs in this country got together to form the British Canoe Union (BCU) in an attempt to organise and develop the sport. The BCU remains the governing body today, and is the driving force behind the promotion of canoeing activities, competitions (regional, national and international) and training. The BCU also helps to provide and increase access to the waterways of the British Isles for canoeists.

After the Second World War, flat water racing was overtaken in popularity by **slalom canoeing**, which uses fast moving, white water. The term 'slalom' was taken from the equivalent activity in skiing. To many newcomers, this was far more exciting than flat water activities and the growth in numbers of people taking part was aided by the availability of reasonably cheap canoe-building kits. This meant that schools, clubs and even the home enthusiast could make and own a canoe. Other factors at this time, such as increased numbers of car owners, better roads, higher wages and more leisure time resulted in the sport becoming available to more people than ever before. It became easy to carry a couple of rigid canoes on the roof rack of a car, so causing a decline in the popularity of the folding canoe.

With the rise in popularity of slalom racing, came changes in canoe design. A sprint canoe needed to be long and narrow for speed, whereas a slalom canoe required greater manoeuverability, so it was flatter and wider.

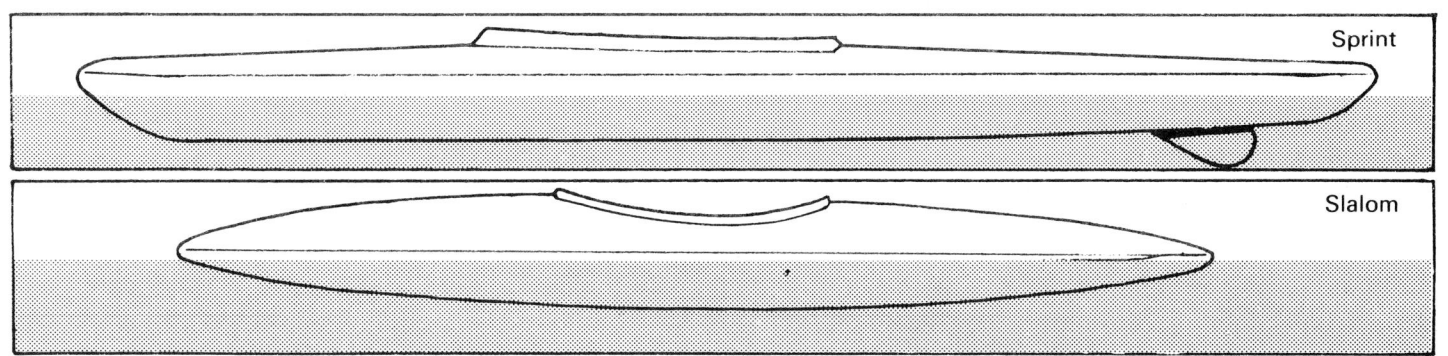

CANOEING

In the 1960s, the sport of canoeing really 'took off' with the introduction of canoes made from glass-fibre reinforced plastics (GRP or **fibre-glass**). It became possible, for the first time, to mass-produce canoes from a mould. Fibre-glass has several advantages:
1. It is light.
2. Canoes made from this are easy to carry.
3. It is easy to repair.
4. Fibre-glass canoes are relatively simple to make and therefore reasonably cheap.

The result was a huge growth in the number of canoe clubs, who could now make and repair their own fleets of canoes. Also, with fibre-glass, many different designs of canoe could be made and tested. This led to the growth of the specialist sports—surf canoeing, canoe sailing, wild water canoeing and, most recently, canoe polo, which now has regional and national leagues.

The state of the sport today

Today, almost every town has a canoe club and most schools have access to canoes or a local education authority outdoor pursuits centre, where water-based activities are practised. It could be said that the sport has become available to almost everyone in the country. Each year, more people are experiencing and taking-up some aspect of canoeing. In terms of the skill and talent of its canoeists, Britain is amongst the best in the world, and our facilities for training and access to water are improving all the time. One of the main reasons behind this is the continued work of the BCU and the other three national canoe associations. The most recent development has been the opening, in 1986, of the artificial slalom and wild water course at Holme Pierrepont, near Nottingham. This offers training and competition facilities and is situated alongside the existing flat water lake, where the 1981 world sprint championships were held.

Exercise 2
The work of the BCU is the main reason for the continued growth in modern day canoeing. Contact the BCU (address on page 136) in order to find out:
1. How to join, including cadet membership for under 17s
2. Addresses of local clubs
3. Regional information about events and training in all the main canoeing sports

You should also obtain a copy of their *Guide to the Waterways of the British Isles* for information about local rivers. You will need this publication to help you with some of the other work in this Chapter.

Exercise 3
Briefly explain the developments in the sport of canoeing which correspond to each of the following dates.
1 mid 1800s 2 1920/30s 3 1945/50s
4 1960s 5 today

1.2 Where to canoe

Many people begin canoeing in a swimming pool. Basic safety and paddling skills can be learned in a controlled, clean and, usually, warm environment. You will find that canoeing on rivers, lakes, canals or the sea is totally different. Outside, the main problem you will be faced with will be that of obtaining **access** to the waterways. For the canoeist, access means two things:
1. being able to get to and from the waterside (i.e. access routes across land to the bank or shore)
2. obtaining permission to use a particular stretch of water.

In Britain, almost all waterways and the surrounding land are privately owned. This means that as a canoeist you have no right of access to most waterways, and even

WHERE TO CANOE

if you do have permission to go on to a stretch of water, you may not be able to get to it with your canoe.

Agreements have been reached in some cases and a few stretches of water are 'free' to canoe, but even so, access is a very real problem for most people. The BCU has an access advisory committee and through its regional officers, negotiates with water and land owners to gain access for canoeists and generally watches out for possible problems. (Note that in Scotland, due to differences in the legal system, the position regarding access differs. Advice should be sought from the Scottish Canoe Association.)

Although there are exceptions, a simple rule should be remembered when asking the question 'Have I got the right to canoe here?'

If the waterway is tidal—**Yes**, you can canoe.
If it is not tidal —**No**, you cannot canoe without permission.

Let's now look in more detail at each of the following waterways: canals, lakes, rivers, estuaries and the sea.

Canals

Most canals in Britain are owned by the British Waterways Board (BWB) and a licence is needed before you are allowed to canoe on them. However, since 1985, a joint scheme between the BWB and the BCU now automatically provides BCU members with a licence to use the canals.

Lakes

Some lakes are 'free'. These are usually in National Parks or where county councils and water authorities have joined together to set up 'water parks'. In most cases, however, you should assume that the lake belongs to someone and that permission is needed before launching your canoe.

Canals provide opportunities for safe canoeing

CANOEING

Rivers

Rivers which are not affected by the tides or the sea are nearly all privately owned. There are only a few 'free' river stretches (e.g. parts of the Thames, Severn and Wye) but even here, this does not give you the right of access to the river banks, for which permission must be sought from the land owners. Some rivers are totally closed to canoeists—these usually run through estates with private fishing rights. However in Scotland and much of Europe, the law of trespass is rather different. Here, most rivers are legally available. It is hoped that England and Wales will adopt a similar policy in the near future. Even so, whether permission has been given or is not required, courtesy should always be shown to land owners and other water users, particularly fishermen who usually have to pay a lot to use the water. Failure to do so could result in permission to use the water being withdrawn, so spoiling other canoeists' enjoyment.

Another factor which affects the number of rivers that are available for canoeing are the properties of the river itself—its speed of flow, obstacles and potential dangers. All rivers are different, and every one changes according to the time of year and amount of water in it. There is an International Rough Water System which grades rivers according to their difficulty. The grades range from I to VI in the following way:

Grade	Description
I	Easy
II	Medium
III	Difficult
IV	Very difficult
V	Exceedingly difficult
VI	Absolute limit of difficulty

Beginners are well advised to stick to rivers graded as I or II or they may find themselves facing dangers they are not capable of dealing with (e.g. difficult rapids, eddies and whirlpools). This Chapter is designed to enable you to canoe safely on rivers up to level II.

Estuaries and the sea

An estuary is the part of a river that runs into the sea and which is subject to the movement of the tides. All tidal water in Britain belongs to the Crown, and so everyone has the right to use it without permission. It is easy to recognise tidal water around the coasts, but how far does it extend up a river? Your OS map will help here, because it shows the upper tidal limits of all estuaries by colouring the river banks black; non-tidal areas of rivers have blue banks.

Water is used for many different activities

Exercise 4

Using your OS mountain map:
1 Locate the bridge over the Afon Cefni at Grid reference 457 727. Notice how the river ceases to be tidal at the bridge.
2 Give the grid references of the upper tidal limit of two other rivers on the map.

Exercise 5
Using your local OS map and the *Guide to the Waterways of the British Isles,* locate your nearest canoeable grade I/II river, then:
1 In preparation for a short trip, put together a log of the route to and from given points, noting where you need to gain permission.
2 Draw a sketch map of the route, adding information on access and navigation.

1.3 Types of canoeing

There are many canoeing activities: some are purely leisure-time recreational pursuits—such as touring and canoe camping—whereas others are sports in their own right, having national and world championships. We shall look in more detail at each of the following sports:
1 Rough water —wild water and slalom
2 Placid flat water—sprint and marathon
3 Surf —surf canoeing
4 Swimming pool —canoe polo

1 Rough water sports

Slalom and wild water racing take place on sections of rough—or **white**—water. Courses are usually on fast-flowing mountain rivers, below weirs or on specially constructed artificial streams (like the one at Holme Pierrepont near Nottingham). Major competitions take place on courses which are graded IV or V.

A wild water competition is simply a straight race against the clock down a section of river. Events are usually held in the winter to make use of the swollen and torrent-like streams, which provide faster conditions.

Slalom, which gets its name from ski racing, consists of a course marked out by **gates** which a competitor must pass through in a given order and direction (forward or reverse). A gate consists of a pair of poles strung over the river which dangle down to just above the water level. Courses normally have between 25–30 gates, including at least four reverse gates. Competitors must pass between the poles of each gate without touching either one with the canoe, paddle or body. Penalty seconds are added to the time for each touch as follows:

Touching one pole—add 5 seconds
Missing gate —add 50 seconds

Each competitor makes two timed runs down the course but is disqualified for that run if he/she capsizes and leaves the canoe.

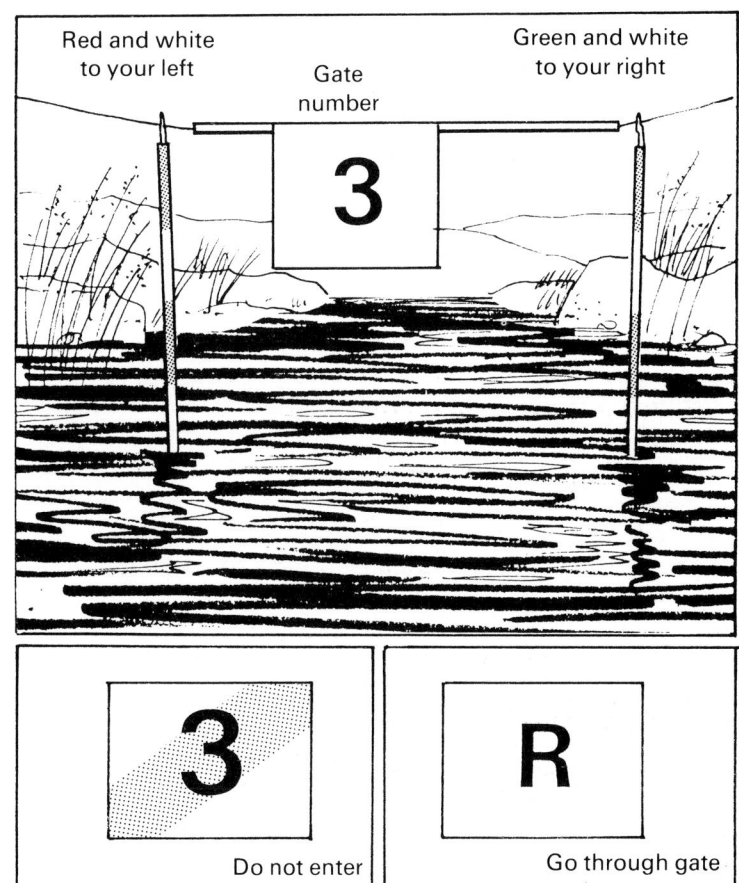

CANOEING

2 Placid (flat) water sports

Placid (or flat) water is found on larger rivers, estuaries, lakes and canals. The lowlands of the south and eastern parts of England have little in the way of white water but plenty of flat water, so this is where sprint racing, in particular, is most popular. Races usually take place on straight courses of 500 m to 10 km. The aim is to get from the start to finish as quickly as possible. A variety of canoes are used: K1, K2 and K4 as well as C1 and C2.

Most recently, marathon racing has developed as a sport, offering the opportunity for canoeists of all abilities to take part in a competitive event. For this reason, the sport is particularly suitable for schools and youth clubs, and local and regional events have become very popular. The best known marathon held in this country is probably the 125 mile Devizes to Westminster race which takes place every Easter.

3 Surf

Canoe surfing is similar to board surfing and is probably the wettest of canoe sports. Competition in Britain usually takes place in the winter, when there is a better chance of finding some good surfing waves. The aim is to first canoe out from the beach, through the broken wave (or **soup**), to take up a position beyond the point where the waves begin to break. Then the surfers choose a wave which they judge will break just as it reaches them. They then give a couple of paddle strokes and try to ride the wave all the way to the beach, 'reading' it all the time in order to keep as close to the breaking section as possible. It's as simple as that! Capsizes are frequent since canoes tend to loop backwards very easily. The competition is judged on a surfer's style and technical ability on each wave.

4 Swimming pool

Canoe polo is played by two teams of five canoeists and is based on the game of water polo. The teams line up along their goal lines and the ball—a size 5 plastic football—is thrown into the middle of the pool by the referee. The object is to score as many goals as possible in the time allowed. After each goal has been scored, the players line up along their goal lines again.

Paddles can be used to stop the ball in the air and draw it along the water, but at no time should they be used to actually propel the ball. Each player must pass the ball within three seconds of receiving it. The game is becoming increasingly popular with canoeists and it has a fully-developed league system, with the national finals held every February during the National Canoe Exhibition at Crystal Palace.

Canoe polo is popular and fun

> *Exercise 6 — Project on canoeing Part 1*
> To be linked with Exercise 7. Choose one of the sports mentioned above (or one you discovered in Exercise 1) and find out more about it. Use the addresses given on page 136, the local canoe club and your library to answer the following points.
> 1 Describe the sport.
> 2 Explain how it is run. Are there national/regional events or leagues? What happens at international level, e.g. Olympics/world championships?
> 3 What happens in a competition?
> 4 Who takes part? Who are the champions and how do they train?

1.4 Types of canoe

The modern kayak comes in a variety of shapes and designs. Before looking more specifically at the specialist canoes used in each of the main sports and activities, you need to become familiar with the basic canoe design.

1 What is a canoe made from?

The majority of modern canoes are made from fibre glass—a glass-fibre mat is moulded into shape and treated with resin to form a strong structure. A similar, but lighter, alternative is polyester cloth. Other possibilities include plastic canoes (sometimes called 'Tupperware boats'). These are strong and they bend on impact, rather than crack as glass-fibre canoes tend to. Because of this durability, plastic canoes are ideal for beginners or groups such as schools, where maintenance needs to be kept to a minimum. Their popularity is likely to increase in the future.

2 What are the main parts of a canoe?

You should become familiar with the following features and parts of a canoe.

(a) Footrest This is an essential part because pushing your feet against it allows strong and efficient paddling, and it also stops you being catapulted out of the boat or jammed down into the front end if you hit something at speed. Most footrests are adjustable so that you can find the correct position before setting off.

(b) Buoyancy Canoes, when waterlogged, will sink! Buoyancy is added to prevent this. There are a number of ways of giving a canoe buoyancy. These include:
  (i) built-in polystyrene blocks, which have the added advantage of providing extra support for the hull
  (ii) adding sections of polyurethane foam at both ends
  (iii) air bags made from PVC, with inflation tubes

(c) Toggles These are present not just for carrying purposes but also to give you something to hold onto should you end up in the water!

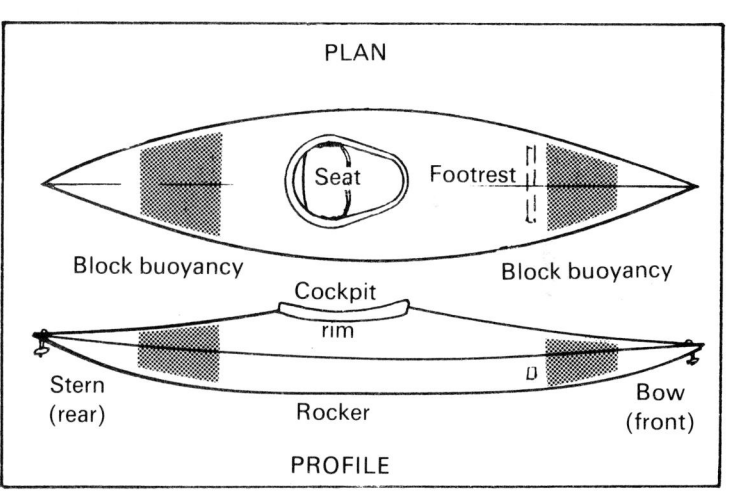

3 The canoe's shape

The shape of a canoe can be considered in three ways: in profile (side-on view), in plan (viewed from above) and in cross-section (as if sliced in half).

(a) Profile shape

When you look at a canoe in profile, you see its **keel**, which usually curves upwards slightly at the stern and bow. This shape is called a **rockered keel** (or rocker for short). A canoe with a rocker can be turned from side to side more easily than one with a straight keel, because the front and rear of the canoe are clear of the water therefore there is less resistance to movement. The greater the upward curve at the stern and bow, the easier the canoe is to turn.

(b) Plan shape

The plan view of a canoe shows the length and width clearly. In general, the longer and narrower a canoe is, the faster and easier it is to paddle in a straight line. However, a narrow canoe is difficult to turn and is unstable. Wider canoes are always more stable and manoeuvrable, but slower, due to increased water resistance arising from the greater area of keel in contact with the water.

(c) Cross-section shape

The cross-section view of a canoe clearly shows the shape across the boat's width. It is the underwater shape which is of most interest to us and there are two extreme types of shape. One is U-shaped, having a flat bottom without a keel line. The other is V-shaped, with a sharp bottom and a strongly pronounced keel. Most canoes fit somewhere in between these two types.

We can now look at some specific canoe designs in terms of their plan, profile and cross-section.

The swimming pool canoe

With the increased use of swimming pools as a place in which to develop canoeing skills, it became necessary to design a small, short, but stable craft that would be more suitable for this use. The Baths Advanced Trainer (BAT for short) has now become widely accepted and used and has helped with the growth of canoe polo.

The slalom canoe

The old style slalom canoe is simply a larger version of the BAT. It is good in most conditions, being stable and easy to turn but, because it has little or no keel line, it remains slow and difficult to keep in a straight line over longer distances on lakes or the sea. Modern types of this canoe have been designed with rockered keels so that the bow and stern which are clear of the water line can be ducked under the poles of the gates in competition. The hull remains flat to provide a high degree of manoeuvrability.

The sprint racing canoe

Sprint racing requires speed in a straight line, therefore these canoes are longer, thinner and they have well-pronounced keel lines to keep them running straight. A racing canoe would be of little use in anything other than flat water.

Exercise 7—Project on canoeing Part 2
(A continuation of work started in Exercise 6.)
For your chosen canoe sport, find out about:
5 Canoe designs
6 Specialist equipment
Information catalogues, etc. can be obtained from mountain/outdoor adventure shops, the *Yellow Pages*—Boats and Small Craft section and Exhibitions, such as the National Canoe Exhibition held in February each year at Crystal Palace, London. The BCU/local canoe club will also provide details.

BASIC SKILLS

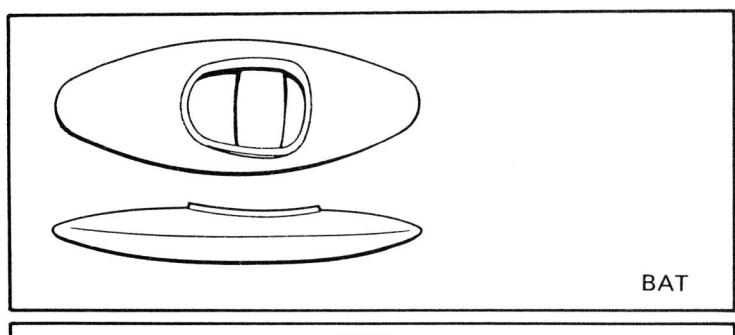
BAT

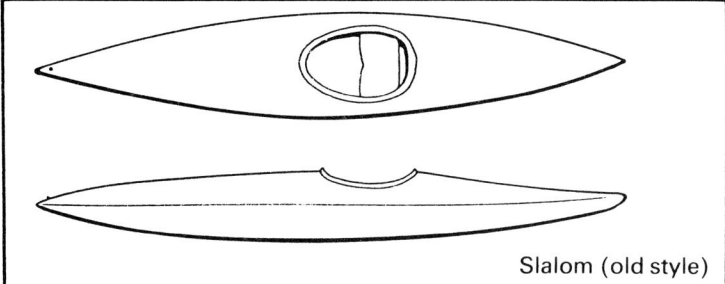
Slalom (old style)

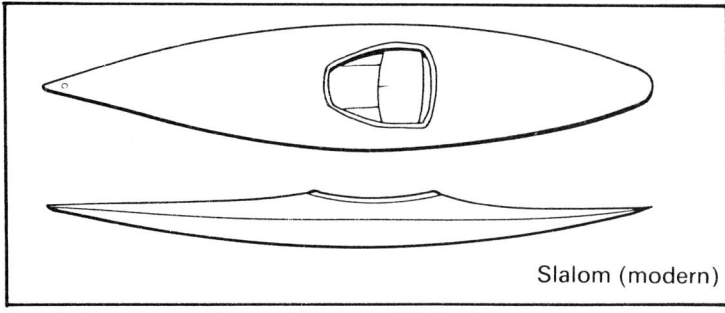
Slalom (modern)

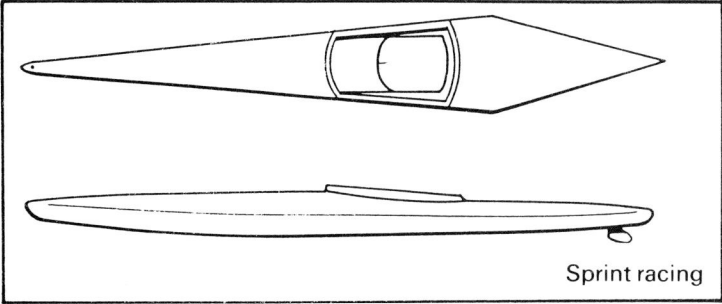
Sprint racing

2 BASIC CANOEING SKILLS

This Section is designed to introduce you to the basics of kayak canoeing under the guidance of your teacher/instructor. We begin by looking at personal equipment and clothing. Then we consider the all-important safety aspects, followed by basic paddling strokes and finally, more general placid water techniques. This work should enable you to develop confidence and gain experience on the shallow, calm water of the swimming pool and placid water rivers, lakes and canals. It will also prepare you for the more advanced deep water skills introduced in Section 3.

2.1 Equipment and clothing

Ready for the water

For comfort and safety reasons, you should always be properly dressed and equipped, no matter where you are paddling. You need a helmet, life-jacket/buoyancy aid, paddle and spray cover, as well as your own personal clothing.

1 Personal clothing

'What to wear' depends upon where you are canoeing (indoors or outdoors) and whether you wish to make use of any specialist clothing that is available.

(a) Indoor pools

When working in a warm indoor pool, you need only wear your normal swimming costume. However, if your canoe is scratchy or rubs—and glass-fibre often does—then you will find that a T-shirt and tracksuit bottoms become a useful addition.

(b) Outdoor waterways

Canoeing outside means, for all but a few weeks in the year, being prepared for cold weather and cold water. As for the other outdoor activities in this book, this means wearing (i) inner clothes to keep you warm, and (ii) an outer shell to help you stay dry. However it is also important to remember that whatever you wear must be suitable for swimming in.

Inner clothes checklist
swimming costume
rugby shirt or non-cotton T-shirt
one or two jumpers
tracksuit bottoms
socks
training shoes or pumps

Outer clothes checklist
waterproof 'cag'
gloves

(c) Specialist clothing

If you decide at a later stage that canoeing is the sport for you, then it is advisable to invest in either a **wet** or a **dry suit**. Wearing a wet suit has proved to be the easiest way of keeping warm, and is used in a whole variety of water sports. There are a large number of styles of wet suit but they all work on the same simple idea: tight-fitting neoprene, 3–6 mm thick, insulates the body by allowing small amounts of water to find its way inside, where it is quickly warmed up by the body's heat. The resulting insulation is simple but effective. Loose-fitting suits do not work at all, because too much water enters, which makes the wearer cold.

For canoeing purposes, you need a suit which does not restrict arm or shoulder movement when paddling. The Long John type, for example, is a one-piece suit without arms. An alternative is the dry suit. This, as its name implies, keeps you dry. It is worn loosely over inner clothes and is sealed at the ankles, wrists and neck.

2 Helmet

A canoeing helmet is light and colourful with holes in it to allow water to drain out easily. It is sensible to wear one when on flowing water, to protect your head from clashes with rocks, banks or even other canoes and paddles.

Canoeing helmets have drainage holes

BASIC SKILLS

3 Life-jacket/buoyancy aid

Your canoe will have built-in buoyancy to keep it afloat. Your own buoyancy can be improved upon by wearing a life-jacket or some other buoyancy aid.

(a) Life-jacket

If you capsize, a life-jacket will help to keep your head above the water level, even if you are unconscious. Life jackets consist of an air bag put on over your head and worn on your chest, secured by a harness. They can be inflated to provide more buoyancy by blowing into the one-way valve.

It is important that life-jackets are worn properly. They should not be loose, and all designs should conform to the British Standard number 3595 (look out for the Kite Mark which is printed on all approved garments). Although particularly valuable for inexperienced water-users, a life-jacket does have the disadvantage of being bulky, so restricting arm movement when paddling. This is why experienced canoeists often prefer to wear a buoyancy aid instead.

(b) Buoyancy aid

This is not nearly as good as a life-jacket at keeping your face above the water level, and it will not float you the right way up if you are unconscious, but it does help to keep you afloat generally. It consists of slim, built-in foam strips or air-sacs which are contained in a waistcoat that can be zipped up at the front.

Exercise 8

1 Draw and label a life-jacket (BSS 3595).
2 Practise putting on a life-jacket. Make sure the buckle or strap is fastened properly. When it's on, put your hand under the front and lift—if the life-jacket moves up to your chin, it is not fastened tightly enough. Pull it from side to side as well—it should not be too loose.

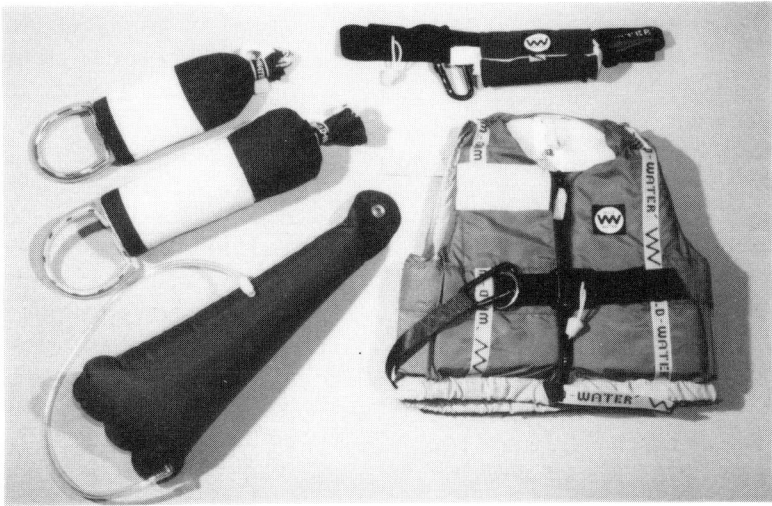

A life-jacket and some buoyancy aids

CANOEING

4 Paddle

A paddle is a very important item of canoeing equipment. No matter what type of canoeing you do, you will need a paddle to be able to move and turn. Paddles also provide support to keep you upright on the water. For kayaking, a **double-bladed paddle** is used.

Paddles can be wooden, but more usually they consist of plastic blades at each end of a shaft made from aluminium and covered in plastic. **Driprings** help to stop water travelling down the shaft to wet your hands and arms. The blades are fitted at right-angles to each other. This arrangement is called **feathering** and is so designed to reduce the wind resistance of the blade which is not in the water when paddling. The blade itself can be flat or curved (spoon shaped). It is best to use the first type when learning, although curved blades offer advantages for the more experienced paddler.

Exercise 9—Getting the feel of a paddle

1. To check that your paddle is the right length, stand it up in front of you. You should be able to curl your fingers over the top blade, as shown below.

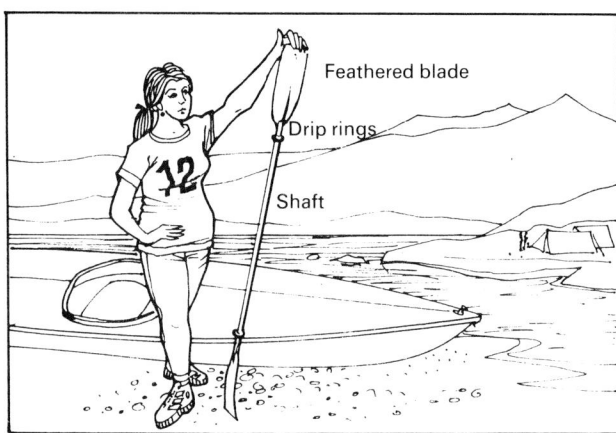

2. To get the correct hand spacing on the shaft of the paddle, copy the bottom diagram. If you have drip-rings, remember to push them to the outside of your hands.

3. You are now ready to find out which hand controls the paddling action. Usually, right-handed people grip and twist the shaft with that hand, allowing their left hand to turn one way then the other as each blade dips in and out of the water. Try this test: Following on from 2 above, hold the paddle out in front, with the right hand blade facing you. Push it out as if to send it into the water on the right ahead of you. Pull it back until it reaches your side, then repeat the motion with the left blade on the left side. If your *right* hand grips and twists as your left hand lets the shaft turn around, you are *right hand controlled*. If your *left* hand does the work, you are *left hand controlled*.

4. A flat-bladed paddle can be used by both right and left-handed canoeists, but a paddle with curved blades cannot. You must find out which hand a curved-bladed paddle is designed for before you use it. Hold the paddle as if you are checking its length (see 1 above), then place the hollow face of the bottom blade on the ground against your toes. If the hollow face of the upper blade is facing right, then it is a right hand paddle. If it's to the left, you have a left hand paddle.

BASIC SKILLS

5 Spray cover

This piece of equipment will be used in Section 3. A spray-cover (or spraydeck) helps to keep water out of the canoe by fitting tightly around your waist and the rim of the cockpit. This seals the inside of the canoe and also keeps you warm. You should not use a spray-cover in the early stages, but later on it allows a variety of rescue skills to be performed so that if you do capsize, you can be brought upright without having to come out of the canoe.

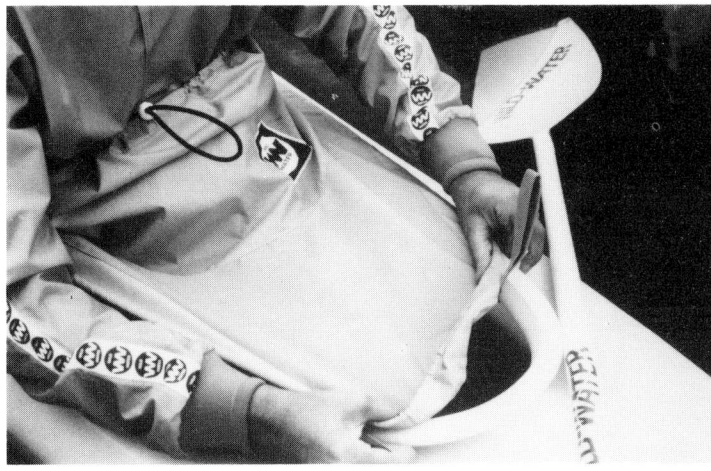

Securing the spray cover

2.2 Basic safety aspects

There are three basic safety procedures canoeists must be familiar with:
 1 How to get in and out of the canoe safely
 2 The capsize drill
 3 How to empty the water from the canoe

These can and should be learned before even thinking about using a paddle. Your teacher/instructor will organise you into groups of at least two or three, with one in the canoe and the others in the water to help, support and assist when necessary. It is vital to practise what to do, to be sensible and to enjoy the water so that you are not put off at this early stage.

1 How to get in and out

The cockpit area of a canoe looks rather small, but it is perfectly safe even for tall or large people. Getting in and out can be practised on dry land first, if necessary.

Position the canoe alongside the edge of the pool or bank. Face the bow (the front end) and sit down on the back of the cockpit. Slide your legs into the cockpit and then sit down. If you can't feel the footrest, you will need to adjust it. To get out, reverse the procedure: draw up your feet until your knees touch your chest. A roll forward will then enable you to stand up.

Slide your legs into the cockpit and sit down

2 Capsizing

Don't worry about your first capsize. It's not as frightening as you may think. Both you and your canoe will be upside down. If you were held in that position on dry land, you would of course soon drop out, head first. In water, falling out is far less traumatic because the water cushions your fall.

CANOEING

Exercise 10—Capsize drill
Hand paddle away from the side of the pool, taking your friends with you, then follow these three stages:
  (i) *Get ready* Lean forward and put your hands on the deck in front of you. Then overbalance to the side and roll over.
  (ii) *Get calm* Still leaning forward, bang hard on the bottom of the canoe three times to signal to everyone else that you have capsized. Then count to three yourself (say 'And-one-and-two-and-three').
  (iii) *Get out* Still leaning forward, put your hands onto the side of the cockpit and push. You will lift off the seat and slide out. The movement is similar to a forward roll.

3 Emptying the canoe

After having capsized, get into the habit of staying with the canoe—keep it upside down until you are ready to empty it. As long as the cockpit is below the water level, the air trapped inside will keep the canoe afloat.

The best method for emptying canoes in swimming pools is to work in pairs: one taking the bow and the other the stern of the upturned canoe. One of the pair should bend his/her knees and lift their end up. If the canoe is twisted, the water will pour out. Then the other end should be lifted and twisted. This see-saw/twisting action will empty the canoe. When all the water has been removed, turn the canoe the right way up and replace it on the water. Don't slam it down onto the water—this can crack the glass-fibre.

Emptying the canoe

A quicker method, using just one person, is to push an end of the canoe on to the side of the pool and lift the other end up and down, removing the water. Then turn it over and get back in. However if the canoe is full of water, it will be very heavy and a more careful approach is necessary. Trying the see-saw technique could result in breaking the canoe across its middle. Before see-sawing, you should go to the side of the upturned canoe, take hold of the cockpit rim and lift it up a little way out of the water so that water inside begins to leave. When enough has poured out, turn it upside down again. Then continue as before.

Exercise 11
1 Under instruction from your teacher/instructor, practise getting into a canoe, hand paddling, capsizing and emptying until it becomes automatic.
2 *Rafting up* One person hand-paddles to the middle of the pool and waits for the others to join them to form a raft.

3 Hand paddling relay race Hand-paddle to one end, capsize and swim with the canoe back to your team. Empty the canoe before the next person starts.

2.3 Basic paddling strokes

We can now consider making use of the canoe paddle. Paddling strokes are important skills. They are the basis of good canoeing. Basic strokes include:
1 Paddling forwards
2 Stopping
3 Paddling backwards
4 Turning
5 Moving sideways

1 Paddling forwards

The blade should be put into the water as near to the bow (front end) as possible. Pull the blade towards you and when it reaches a point level with your body, flick it out and repeat the stroke on the other side. The canoe won't move forward in a straight line: as the paddle is pulled through the water on one side, the bow will move slightly towards the other side. By repeating the stroke on the other side, the bow is sent back, and so on. The canoe therefore moves forward in a zig-zag. The smaller the zig-zag the better, but this takes some practice. At first, you will find that your zig-zags are very large.

Moving forwards. Push at approximately shoulder level

CANOEING

> *Exercise 12*
> 1. Improve your zig-zag technique by aiming for a marker straight ahead of you.
> 2. Improve your paddling by using both arms to take the paddle through the water. When you are pulling with one arm, you should also push with the opposite arm, and vice versa. This method is much less tiring.
> 3. Use your footrest: push with the foot opposite the blade that is in the water. When the right hand blade is in the water, push with the left foot, and vice versa.

2 Stopping

The simplest way to stop yourself from going forwards is to paddle backwards, i.e. do everything in reverse: lean backwards, put the blade in the water behind you and push it forwards. You should be able to stop any forward movement after three or four backwards strokes.

> *Exercise 13 Stopping practice*
> As directed by your teacher/instructor, paddle forwards to get up some speed. After a given point, stop the canoe in as short a distance as possible.

3 Paddling backwards

The technique is the same as for stopping except that to travel backwards, you need to see where you are going. Therefore as well as leaning back, twist your body so that you can look over one shoulder as you put the blade into the water near to the stern. Look forwards on the next stroke to make sure you keep going in a straight line.

> *Exercise 14*
> Repeat Exercise 12 but go backwards instead of forwards.

4 Turning strokes

You will probably find that you have little difficulty in turning the canoe around—you may even do it when you don't really want to! There are a large range of strokes which turn the canoe in different ways. The simplest involves putting the blade into the water and keeping it there. You will find that the canoe will turn towards that side. More positive turns include:
(a) the sweep turn
(b) the low brace turn

(a) The sweep turn

This stroke can be used to turn the canoe to the left or right when you are travelling forwards or backwards. A **forward sweep** is simply an exaggerated version of a forward paddle stroke, where the blade is placed in the water near the bow, then swept out in a backwards arc and withdrawn from the water near the stern. The bow will turn to move in the opposite direction.

Forward sweep turn

Reverse sweep is an exaggeration of a backward paddle stroke which is achieved by placing the blade in the water near the stern, sweeping it forward and taking it out near the bow, resulting in the canoe bow turning towards the side of the sweep.

(b) The low brace turn

The sweep turn can be developed into the **low brace turn** in order to turn more quickly. This is useful if you need to manoeuvre alongside the pool side or a river bank. You begin by making a reverse sweep and as the speed increases, you lean over towards the blade, digging it in deeper in order to turn more quickly. With confidence, you can do this quicker and lean further. At the beginning, you may find this gives you an opportunity to practise your capsize drill as well!

Exercise 15 — Sweep turns
To turn the canoe to face the opposite direction, try doing a forward sweep followed by a reverse sweep on the opposite side.

Exercise 16 — Low brace turns
Your teacher/instructor will position a target for you to canoe towards. Move towards it and when you are close, turn around so that you come alongside the target. As you improve, increase the speed of your approach and turn.

Practising the low brace turn using a target

CANOEING

5 Moving sideways

Making a sideways movement is often necessary, especially when manoeuvring to come alongside other canoes or the side of the pool. The easiest way to do this is to use the **draw stroke** (which 'draws' the canoe sideways). The paddle is placed into the water on the side to which the movement is required. Next, pull the blade of the paddle towards the side of the canoe, then twist it so that it slices out of the water. Repeat the movement as often as necessary. As you get better, try to increase the amount you lean over towards the blades, but don't let the blade go under the canoe or you will probably follow it!

Exercise 17—Draw stroke
Practise the draw stroke by moving sideways to the edge of the pool and then back out towards the middle again. Try this on both sides of the pool.

Exercise 18—Rafting-up with paddles
1 One person waits in the middle of the pool for the others to join him/her using any of the following skills to come alongside:
  (a) low brace
  (b) from behind paddling forwards
  (c) from in front paddling backwards
2 With the paddles placed across the decks and the canoeists holding the adjoining cockpit rim as shown in the diagram on page 123, the people on the ends can use their paddles to move the whole raft forwards, backwards or around (if one paddles forwards and the other backwards).
3 When breaking-up, to give each other room to manoeuvre, it is best if the people at each end leave first.

Moving sideways using the draw stroke

2.4 Placid water canoeing

The safety and paddling skills developed so far are aimed at preparing you for kind weather canoeing ventures on placid water (grade I) rivers, lakes and canals. But before leaving the comfort of the pool, there are some things you should know about canoeing on open water.

1 Golden rules

Keep close together.
Keep to the pace of the slowest canoeist.
Don't go out alone (remember these wise words: *less than three there should never be!*).
A capsized canoe will float. Don't try to right it—stay with it unless, that is, it's heading for danger, such as a weir.

2 Basic river knowledge

Your teacher/instructor will take the following points into account when planning your first river trip, and you should be aware of them too.

(a) It is best to stick to downstream paddling. If this can't be avoided (e.g. on trips where you need to return to the place from which you started), then paddle upstream first and return downstream.

(b) Avoid weirs and lock gates, where currents can be difficult and dangerous. (A weir is simply a wall across a river which controls the flow by holding back a mass of water.)

(c) Approach bridges with care. A bridge blocks some of the flow and concentrates it under the archway, so even on slow-moving currents, the speed of water under the archways will increase.

Exercise 19 — A downstream trip
This will be organised by your teacher/instructor. Use the information you collected in Section 1 Exercise 5 to plan your trip on a local river, canal or lake.

---

3 DEEP WATER SKILLS

In Britain, most of the water available for canoeing consists of placid water rivers, lakes and canals. You should have already gained some experience of this type of water.

This Section prepares you for tackling deeper water. Much of this work can take place in a swimming pool. Some safety aspects and rescue techniques are considered first, followed by the introduction of more advanced paddling strokes. The Chapter finishes by considering the technique of rolling.

3.1 Safety in deep water

1 The spray cover

Wearing a spray cover increases the range of canoeing activities that you can take part in, and for much of the work in this Section, it is an essential item of equipment. It allows you, for example, to remain in a capsized canoe so that you can roll yourself back over, once you have learned that technique.

A good spray cover must fit tightly around your waist and around the rim of the cockpit in order to keep water out of the canoe. However, it must also be able to be pulled off quickly in an emergency.

A spray cover is put on in three stages.

(a) Step into the spray cover and pull it up to your waist. Adjust the clip if necessary.

(b) Hold the cover up as you get into the cockpit, otherwise you may sit down on it.

(c) Reach behind and pull the elastic edge of the cover over the rim of the cockpit. Then, using both hands, work towards the front checking that the release strap or loops are on the outside. Also check that nothing else is trapped between the rim and the cover.

Exercise 20 — Spray cover confidence
1 Working on dry land, put on a spray cover. Get into a canoe, fit the cover on and then pull it out and up to get it off. Repeat this.
2 Now try it in water.
3 Now capsize the canoe and add 'Get spray cover off' to the list of 'Gets': (1) GET ready
    (2) GET calm
    (3) GET spray cover off
    (4) GET out

2 Rescues

As you begin to learn more advanced techniques, the likelihood of capsizing increases. Having to get out, empty the canoe and then get back in again can be time consuming and frustrating if it happens more than a few times. Wearing a spray cover gives the canoeist an advantage here, because several procedures can be performed which make correcting a capsize quicker and simpler. The simplest of these is to use breast-stroke movements with your arms in order to 'swim' to the side of the pool without actually leaving the cockpit. Other methods include: (a) the **swimmer-to-canoeist rescue**
(b) the **bow rescue**

In the **swimmer-to-canoeist rescue**, one of the 'spotters' (people watching the others canoe) must reach the upturned canoe. They then reach right over the canoe and take hold of either the cockpit or the canoeist's arm. By leaning back and pulling, they should be able to turn the capsized canoe the right way up. Care should be taken to ensure that the 'spotter' doesn't accidentally cause the canoe to overbalance and capsize in the other direction!

Exercise 21—Swimmer rescue
Capsize and go through the normal 'Get ready, Get calm' stages of the drill, then wait to be rescued by the 'spotter' who should be standing next to your canoe. If, for some reason, you are not rescued, complete the 'Get spray cover off, Get out' stages and ask questions later!

A **bow rescue** requires a little more effort from the capsized canoeist. The first diagram below shows a canoeist awaiting rescue; but instead of the 'spotter' performing the rescue, the bow of another canoe is being manoeuvred into position on one side of the upturned canoe. On feeling the bow, the capsized canoeist grabs hold of it with both hands and, leaning forward, pulls on it in order to roll back up as shown in the second diagram.

Swimmer-to-canoeist rescue

Bow rescue

DEEP WATER SKILLS

> *Exercise 22—Bow rescue*
> Practise this rescue, but be prepared to get out if it does not work at first.

3 Deep water rescue

There will be occasions when you cannot be rescued by a swimmer or the bow of another canoe. The only option in these circumstances is to get out and stay with your upturned canoe until help arrives. A **deep water rescue** is where one canoe, or a couple working together, help to empty and right the upturned canoe in order to get you back into it as quickly as possible. There are several ways of doing this, but probably the simplest are:
  (a) the 'X' method—used when the upturned canoe has very little water inside it.
  (b) the 'TX' method—used when the upturned canoe is swamped with water.

(a) 'X' Method

'X' refers to the shape that is made when the upturned canoe is being emptied see-saw fashion over the foredeck of the rescue canoe. Whilst this is happening, the capsized canoeist should try to look after his or her paddle. S/he should also hold onto the bow of the rescue boat for safety. Once their canoe is emptied and placed alongside, the capsized canoeist can re-enter.

> *Exercise 23—'X' method of deep water rescue*
> 1 Below are four diagrams illustrating the 'X' method of rescue. Draw and explain what is happening in each one.
> 2 Practise this method of rescue in the swimming pool under the direction of your teacher/instructor so that you can perform it with ease and speed.

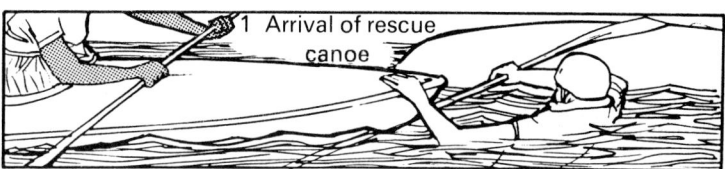
1 Arrival of rescue canoe

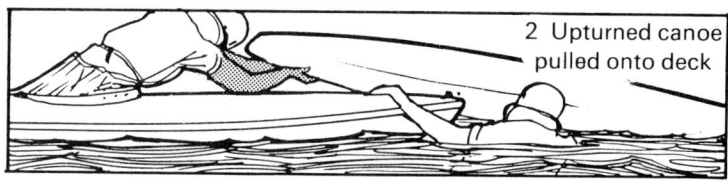
2 Upturned canoe pulled onto deck

3 See-saw to empty

4 Canoes held steady for re-entry

CANOEING

(b) 'TX' Method

This occurs in two stages. First, the 'T' arrangement is adopted. This reduces the amount of water inside the capsized canoe so that the 'X' method can then be followed. The 'T' shape is formed by the rescue and the upturned canoes adopting positions as shown below. The rescuer paddles his or her canoe's bow up to, and inside, the cockpit of the capsized canoe (so making the 'T'). The person in the water pulls their canoe over slightly to help.

This action alone will allow some water to run out, but the canoe is still likely to be heavy, so the person in the water should push their canoe a little further up onto the deck of the rescuing canoe. The canoe can then be emptied using see-saw motions as before. The 'TX' method is useful when the capsized canoe is very heavy with water because the first stage (bow into cockpit) allows some of the water to escape before the canoe has to be pulled up on to the deck of the rescuing canoe.

Exercise 24—'TX' method of deepwater rescue
1. Below are four diagrams relating to the 'T' part of the 'TX' rescue method. Draw them and explain what is happening in each one.
2. Practise this method in the swimming pool but start with canoes that are not swamped with water before tackling the real thing.

3.2 Support strokes

This Section goes a stage beyond the basic paddling strokes discussed in Section 2.3, which prepared you for placid water rivers, lakes and canals. We now consider a simple support stroke, which will help you to avoid capsizing your canoe.

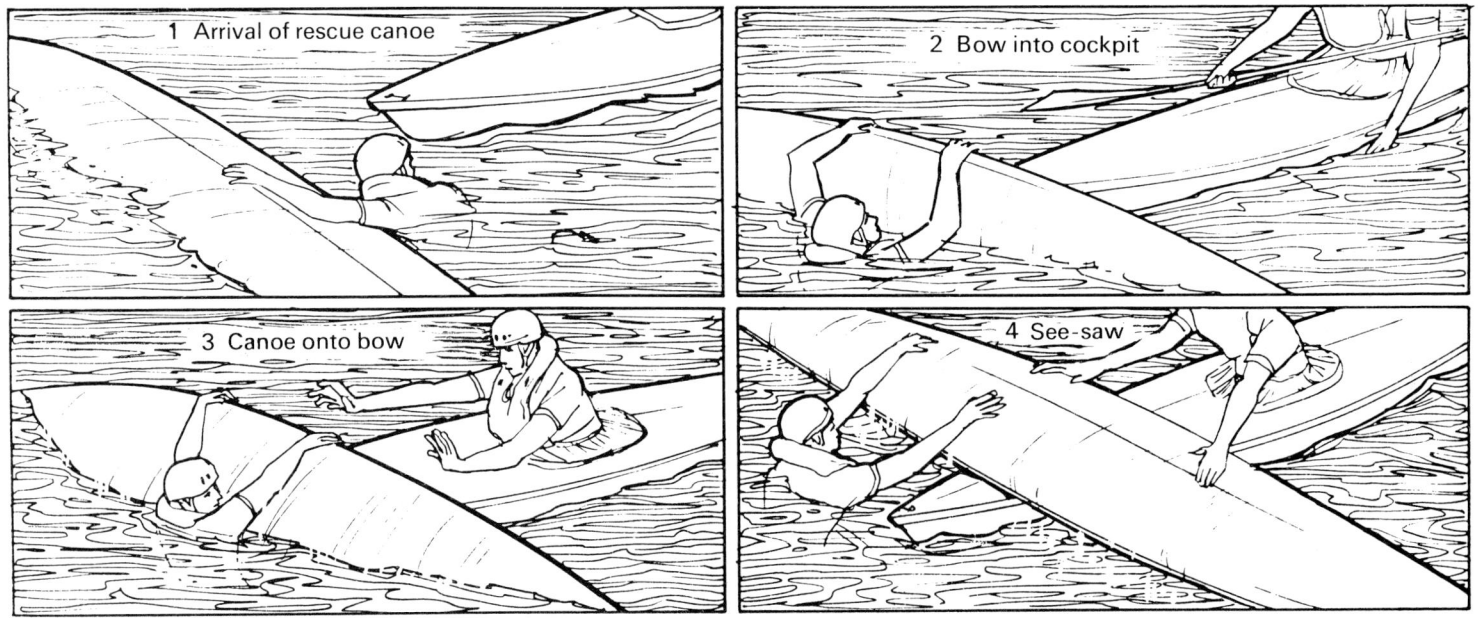

The 'push' support stroke

As the name suggests, this stroke involves pushing the blade of the paddle flat onto the surface of the water in order to prevent a capsize. The following diagrams show this stroke being used in two different situations. The nearer you are to the surface of the water, the more skill you need in order to right your canoe.

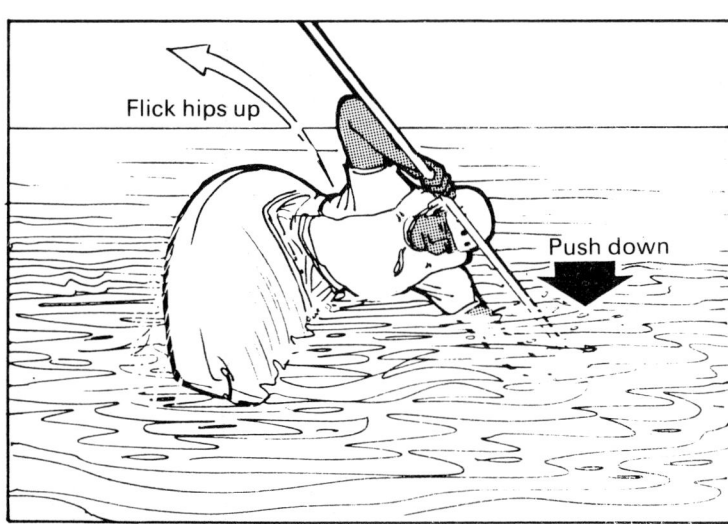

Push support stroke at elbow level (top) and shoulder level (above)

Exercise 25

1 'Wet hand level'   Hold the paddle in the normal way. Reach out to one side and place the blade flat onto the surface of the water. Lift the blade up and and then place it down again—you should be able to feel the resistance coming from the surface of the water. This is what prevents you from capsizing once you have mastered this technique.

2 'Wet elbow level'   This involves over-balancing and reaching out to the side with the paddle. Push down on the blade and throw your hips upwards at the same time. If you do it properly, this will bring you and the canoe back up to the normal position. This hip action is called 'hip flick'.

3 'Wet shoulder level'   As your timing and technique improve, your teacher/instructor will encourage you to lean over further still, so that eventually, you should be able to correct the canoe's position even when your shoulder is almost touching the water.

3.3 Advanced swimming pool skills—rolling

What is rolling?

The 'Eskimo roll' is a very useful skill to learn. It is basically a method of self-rescue in which the paddle is used to correct your position after a capsize. There are several different ways of rolling, and we will look at two.

The **Pawlata**, which gets its name from the Austrian who devised it, is generally considered to be the easiest to learn. The **screw roll**, however, is probably the most useful. It differs only slightly from the Pawlata roll. Other methods, such as the steyr, storm, put across and hand roll are variations which have been developed for specific situations. They are beyond the scope of this Chapter.

There are four stages to get from the Pawlata to the screw roll.

CANOEING

Stage 1—The hip flick

Successful rolling depends on a good hip flick technique. To practise this, you need to use either the bar or ledge at the side of the swimming pool, or the shaft of a paddle held out horizontally by one of the 'spotters'. The sequence of movements is as follows:

1. Hold onto the bar, lean towards it and turn the canoe over.
2. Keeping your head and shoulders in the water, 'throw' your hips up and away from the bar in one quick movement. This should turn the canoe the right way up.
3. Finally push on the bar to raise your head and body, and finish off by leaning your weight on the back of the canoe's deck.

It is important that you turn the canoe using the 'flick' of your hips *before* bringing up your head, shoulders and body—their weight, if brought up too soon, will simply pull the canoe back down into the water.

Exercise 26—Hip flick drill
1. Using the diagrams as your guide, take it in turns to practise the hip flick. Whilst 'spotting', learn and instruct by watching carefully. If the canoeist can't make it up, use the assisted roll to help them (see the swimmer-to-canoeist rescue, Section 3.1).
2. In order to prepare for the complete roll, which requires you to capsize over one side and come up on the other, try leaning forward and going over on the opposite side from the bar. Then find the bar with both hands and repeat the hip flick drill in the normal way, so that you end up leaning backwards on the deck.

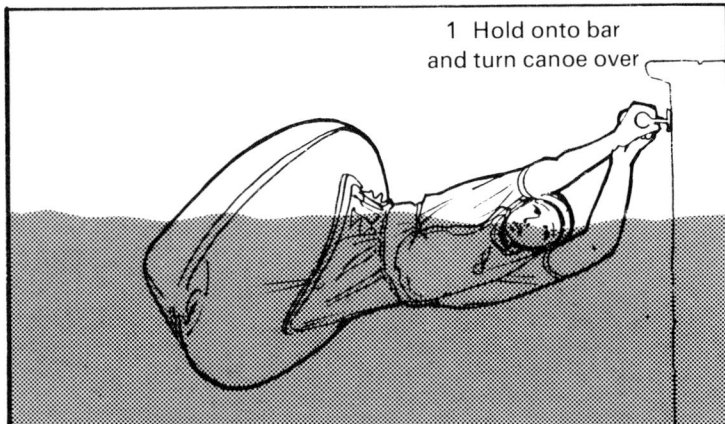

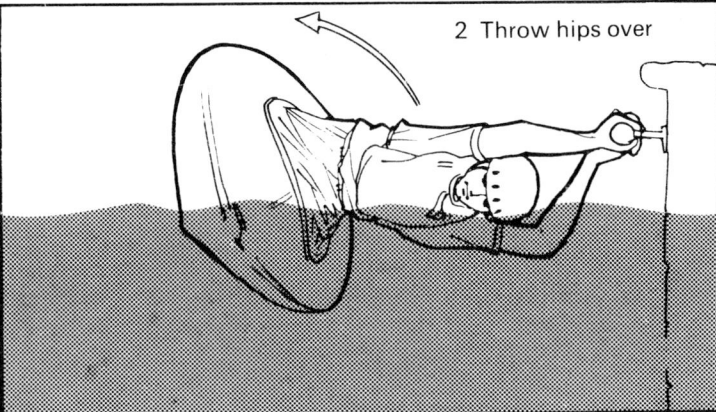

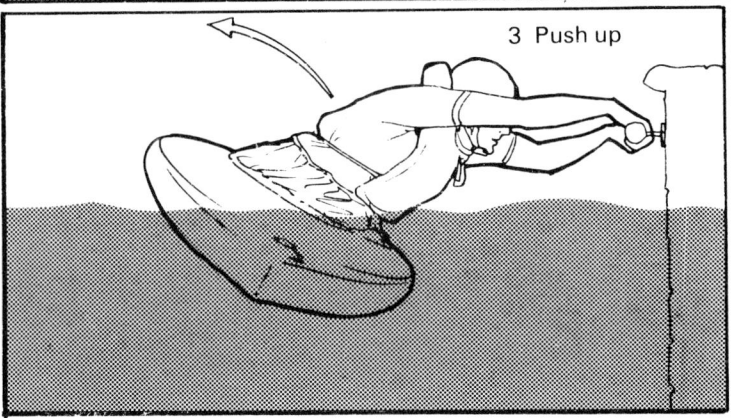

Hip flick practice

Stage 2—Same-side pawlata

Now we combine the use of the paddle with the hip flick. This is similar to the 'push' support stroke described in Section 3.2.

1. Hold the paddle as shown above, with one hand behind the blade. (In this case, it is the canoeist's left hand—but it could just as easily be your right—use whichever feels most comfortable.) The other hand should be in the normal paddling position.
2. Holding the paddle in this way, repeat the 'push' support drill (Section 3.2, Exercise 25), but when you get to the 'wet shoulder level', instead of pushing the blade *down*, sweep it backwards over the surface of the water in order to bring yourself back up.
3. The next step is to fully capsize, leaning forward with the paddle blade pointing towards the bow, on the top of the water. After the 'spotter' has checked that it is angled slightly upwards towards the stern, sweep it backwards in order to turn the canoe. When the blade passes your body, use a hip flick to turn you all the way. Remember to keep your head and shoulders in the water until the canoe is upright and to finish up leaning back.

DEEP WATER SKILLS

Exercise 27—Same-side roll
Work through the above three levels, using a 'spotter' to hold the paddle blade and, if necessary, to walk around as you sweep. (Someone holding the blade provides extra resistance for you to push against.) If you consistently fail, go back to improve your hip flick technique and then try again. If you can do it, congratulations! You are now ready to learn the full Pawlata.

Stage 3—Pawlata roll

A complete roll involves capsizing on one side of the canoe and rolling back up on the other. The sweep and flick motions remain the same, but to practise, you begin on the other side of the canoe (the side opposite the swimming pool bar/ledge). We can divide the practice roll into three stages: Get ready, Get set and Go!

The 'Get ready' stage

The paddle should be parallel to the canoe's length, as shown below. The canoeist is getting ready to go down on the left-hand side and roll up on the right-hand side. Notice that at this stage, the canoeist is leaning slightly forwards. The blade is flat against the boat at the bow and the right-hand wrist is locked, with knuckles pointing downwards. (This puts the blade into the correct position for the 'Get set' stage.) The left hand is holding the rear blade of the paddle. Now the canoe is capsized.

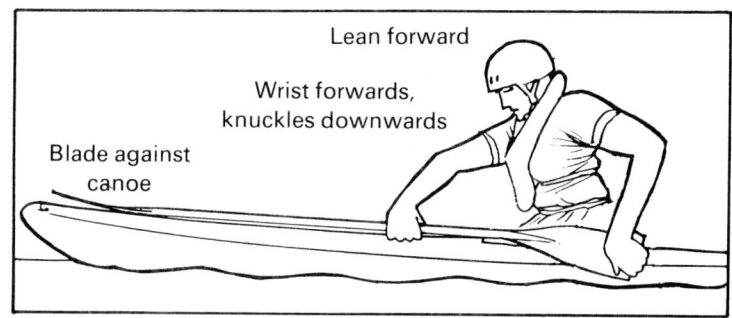

CANOEING

The 'Get set' stage

At this stage, you are underwater and still leaning forwards, holding one paddle blade against the bow. In 'Get set', you must position the blade so that you are ready to make a sweep with it. A 'spotter' can help here by pushing the bow away as you begin to sweep—otherwise, the first time you try it, you could find that you move the paddle the wrong way, and bring the blade underneath the bow by mistake.

The 'Go' stage

Now sweep hard, lean back and flick with your hips to end up leaning back on the deck, the correct way up.

Exercise 28—Pawlata roll

1 Study the following diagram and describe what is happening at each stage.

2 Under the guidance of your teacher/instructor work through the three stages just described. Use a 'spotter' to help you set the blade and to guide it over the surface of the water—but you should be able to pull on the paddle and flick into the correct position by yourself. When you feel confident, try the entire procedure alone.

Common faults when learning to roll include:
1 Pulling the blade under the bow instead of sweeping it in the correct direction.
2 Using the hip flick movement too soon. Let the paddle sweep do the work—then flick.
3 Lifting head and shoulders out of the water before the canoe has turned upright. Remember to lean back on the deck when finishing.

Stage 4—Screw roll

Once you have succeeded with the Pawlata roll, your teacher/instructor will introduce you to the **screw roll**. This technique differs from the Pawlata in only one way: this time you hold the paddle in the normal fashion, not with one hand around the rear blade. This means that you are not able to pull on the paddle quite as strongly, therefore you must have developed a good hip flick technique in order to use a screw roll effectively.

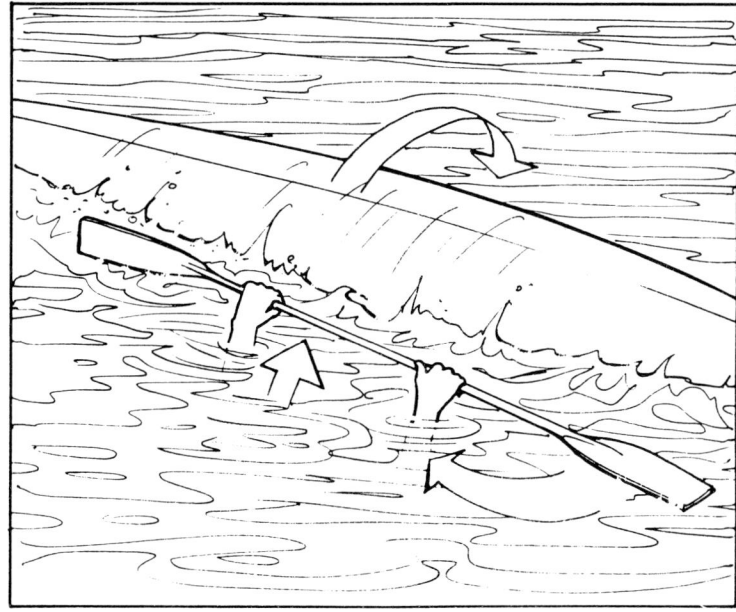

Ready to 'go' for a screw roll

Conclusion

Canoeing involves a whole variety of activities and sports. In this Chapter, we have only been concerned with the kayak, and we have aimed at developing basic placid water skills. Should you wish to progress onto flowing water, you must learn more about how rivers behave, and develop more advanced paddling strokes and river skills. It is advisable, therefore, to join a canoeing club. No matter what type of water interests you, there will be opportunities to visit and take part in events, trips and competitions. You could also enter for the award scheme run by the BCU/SCA.

Important note: Weil's disease

When canoeing on rivers and canals, you should be aware of the risk of the above disease. It is caused by a bacterium which is carried in rats' urine and which is found in slow-moving water and around wet river banks.

Weil's disease can be caught through minor cuts on your skin and feet, or if you do capsize drill or rolling in a river or canal. The symptoms are like those of 'flu, *but this is a much more serious disease*. If you experience 'flu symptoms after canoeing, tell your doctor immediately and mention Weil's disease. (It sounds like 'veal'.)

Useful precautions
1 Avoid capsize drill or rolling in stagnant or slow-moving water.
2 Wash or shower after canoeing.
3 Cover minor scratches on exposed parts of the body with waterproof plaster.
4 Use footwear to avoid cutting feet.

FURTHER INFORMATION

Governing bodies/organisations

British Canoe Union (BCU): The governing body for all aspects of canoeing in this country, including training awards and information relating to courses and regional and local clubs. Membership brings many benefits for the individual, school or family, and includes reduced rates for under 17s and a special one year introductory membership.
Address: British Canoe Union, Flexel House, 45–47 High Street, Addlestone, Weybridge, Surrey KT15 1JV   Telephone: 0932 41341

Other National Association addresses are:
Scottish Canoe Association (SCA), 18 Ainslie Place, Edinburgh, EH3 6AU Telephone: 031 226 4401
Welsh Canoeing Association, 3 Gillian Road, Llandaff, Cardiff, South Glamorgan
Canoe Association of N. Ireland, House of Sport, Upper Malone Road, Belfast, N. Ireland BT9 6LA Telephone: 0232 663154
The Canadian Canoe Association of Great Britain, Honorary Secretary, Gable Cottage, Downs End, Leatherhead, Surrey KT22 8JJ
Irish Canoe Union, c/o Cospoir, Floor 11, Hawkins House, Dublin 2
The Canoe Camping Club (CCC), 25 Waverley Road, S. Norwood, London SE25 4HT

Maps, guides and information about canals

Information Centre, British Waterways Board, Melbury House, Melbury Terrace, London NW1 6JX   Telephone: 01 262 6711

Magazines

Canoe Focus—bi-monthly, free to members of the BCU.
The Canoe Camper—free to members of the Canoe Camping Club.
Canoeist—monthly from newsagents, or direct from publisher: Mrs R. J. Fisher, 13 Wellington Crescent, Banghurst, Basingstoke, Hants RG26 5PF Telephone 07356 2911.

WORKSHEET

1. What does K1 mean?
2. Name five sports in which canoes are used.
3. What do the letters BCU stand for?
4. Write down three differences between kayak and Canadian canoeing.
5. When looking at a river on an OS map:
   (a) How can you tell if it is tidal?
   (b) What does this mean?
6. What do the letters GRP stand for?
7. Explain (a) why paddle blades are feathered,
   (b) how to tell if a paddle is too long or too short for you.
8. A lifejacket and a buoyancy aid do similar jobs.
   (a) In what ways are they different?
   (b) Which is more suitable for canoeing?
9. In surf canoeing, what is the 'soup'?
10. Draw a plan of a swimming pool to show the position of the canoes at the start of a game of canoe polo.
11. What do the letters BAT stand for, and where are you likely to use one?
12. Describe the method used to find out which hand a paddle with curved blades is for.
13. Explain what should happen in each of these phases of the capsize drill: 'Get ready', 'Get calm', 'Get spray cover off', 'Get out'.
14. It is often necessary to move the canoe sideways. What is the technique for doing this called and how does it work?
15. Complete the golden rules of river canoeing.
    (a) Keep.... (b) Keep to the pace...
    (c) Less than... (d) Stay with..., unless it is...
16. Using diagrams, explain how the 'X' method of deep water rescue should be performed.
17. Describe the important points to remember in each of the following stages of performing a roll: 'Get ready', 'Get set', 'Go!'.

The next three questions should be answered together in the form of an essay, so that question 18 becomes the introduction, 19 the main part of the essay and 20 forms the conclusion.

Title: **The Problem of Access to Waterways.**

18. Explain what the word access means to the canoeist.
19. There is a simple rule on access, but the problem is a complex one.
    (a) What is the simple rule?
    (b) Explain the situation for each of the following waterways:
       (i) canal (ii) lake (iii) river (iv) estuary and sea
    (c) Describe the role of the BCU in helping with problems of access.
20. The trespass law in many European countries is rather different to that of England and Wales.
    (a) How does this affect canoeing in Europe?
    (b) Do you think the situation should change in England and Wales?
    (c) Even where permission is not required, how should a canoeist behave?

© Ian Lockren 1988   Permission is given to photocopy the above worksheet without fee for use in the institution by which the book is bought.

APPENDIX A: FIRST AID

It is essential that the leader of any group or party using mountains or waterways has a good working knowledge of first aid. This can be gained by attending one of the many excellent and easy-to-follow courses organised in Britain by the St John's Ambulance Association, the British Red Cross or, in Scotland, the St Andrew's Ambulance Association. It is also just as important that everyone else taking part has at least a basic understanding of what to do in cases of minor (cuts and bruises) and major (life or death) emergency situations, when qualified medical help can be many kilometres and hours away.

This Appendix is intended only as a basic, beginner's course in first aid. You should follow it up by joining a course for further instruction. Alternatively, your teacher/instructor may arrange for experts to visit the school. First aid skills will be useful and valuable in any situation.

What is first aid? Basically, as the name suggests, it is the help that you are able to offer a casualty immediately, at the time of injury. This help could be at one of two levels.

1. With serious injury, it may be a case of keeping the casualty alive while qualified medical assistance is sought.
2. With less-serious injury (e.g. cuts, bruises, strains and sprains), the priority is to relieve the pain and get the casualty home; or, if this is not possible, to make the casualty safe and comfortable whilst qualified assistance is sought.

However, remember that because of the remoteness of many areas of mountain, sea and waterway, *any* outdoor pursuits accident should be treated as serious, and you should follow the advice given in Chapter 2, Section 3.

Serious injury procedure

When dealing with what looks like a serious injury, you should remember to:

1. Check to see if the casualty is conscious.
2. Check for breathing.
3. Check for bleeding.

If the casualty answers questions, then he/she is conscious and breathing. If there is no response to questions, shaking or pinching, then the casualty is unconscious, and the **ABC** action described below should be taken immediately.

A for **airway**   Check the airway (the nose/mouth and throat) which may be blocked by the tongue, vomit or other objects and secretions. Remove any obstructions you see and open the airway by tilting the head back gently: lift the chin with two fingers under it, pressing the forehead backwards with the other hand. This action will allow air into the lungs and may itself re-start breathing.

If the casualty is still not breathing then you must take action to help re-start it.

B for **breathing**   Check for breathing by listening for expired air, or feel for the breathing movements of the lower chest with your hand. If no breathing is detected, immediately start mouth to mouth resuscitation ('The Kiss of Life'). First, pinch the casualty's nose. Breath in and seal the casualty's mouth with your own (or if it is a small child, seal both mouth and nose). Blow carefully into his/her mouth until the chest rises.

If the chest does not rise, it means that the mouth is not sealed properly or that the casualty's head is not tilted back far enough (in which case the tongue might be blocking the airway). Put this right, then try again. Watch for the chest to rise, remove your mouth and then wait for

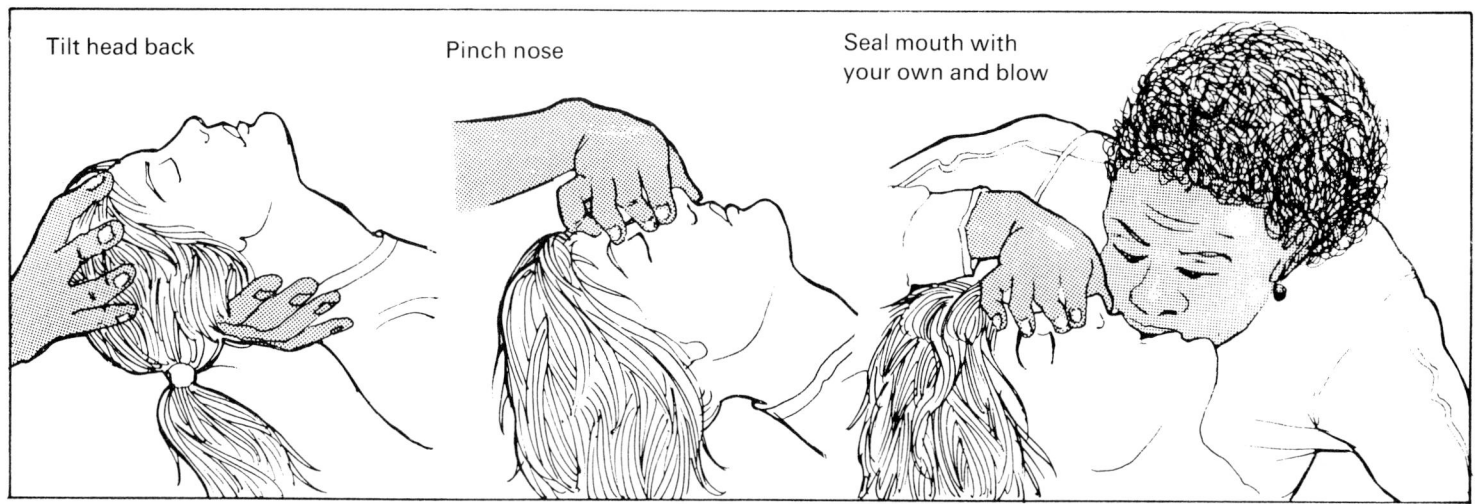

it to fall. Keep blowing into the casualty at your normal rate of breathing.

It is important to combine this summary with supervised practical experience and never to practise on each other.

C for **circulation** This means checking for and, where necessary, controlling bleeding. If the casualty is bleeding, then you should try to stop it by applying pressure to the wound. Some ways of applying pressure are shown on the right.

Tie a clean pad over the wound, secure with a bandage and raise that part of the body if you can. Then apply another bandage on top of the first. In cases of heavy blood loss, lay the casualty down and raise the feet and legs above the level of the heart, to ensure blood flows into the head and brain. Try to avoid contact with the blood but if this is not possible, as in many emergency situations, make sure you thoroughly wash the blood off yourself after treating the casualty.

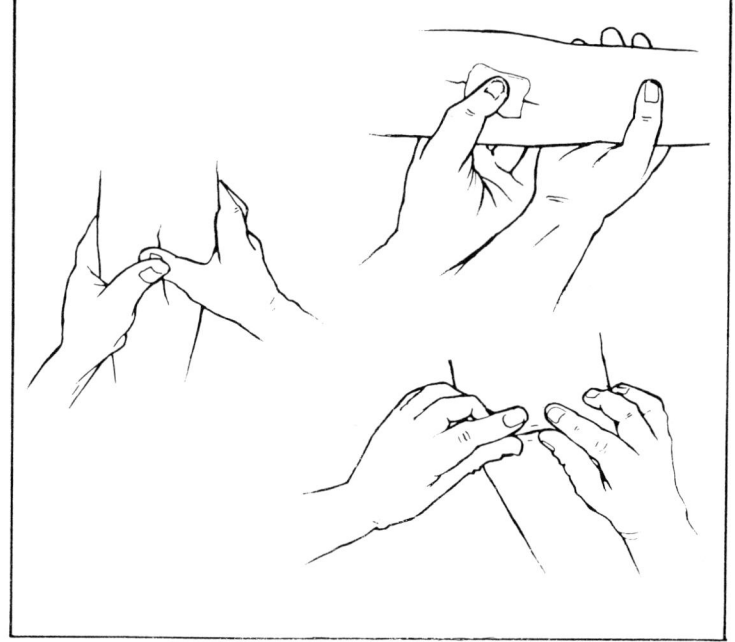

Some methods of arresting bleeding

APPENDIX A

Unconsciousness

After going through the ABC procedure, an unconscious but breathing casualty should be placed in the recovery position. The only exception to this is if a back or neck injury is suspected. In this case, the casualty should only be moved if breathing becomes a problem (e.g. if the breathing is noisy), requiring the airway to be improved.

The method used to move a casualty who is lying on his/her back into the recovery position is shown in the diagrams. If the casualty is lying on his/her side or is face-down, the method should be modified to bring the casualty into the correct position.

Kneel down beside the casualty's chest, then:
1. Place the nearest arm close to his/her side with the hand near the buttock.
2. Cross the far leg over the near one.
3. Bring the other arm across the chest.
4. Support the head and gently pull the casualty onto his/her side towards you, making sure the chin is forward to keep the airway open.
5. Move the top arm into the bent position.
6. Move the top leg into the bent position.
7. Ease the other arm out from under the body.
8. Make sure that he/she is not lying fully on the chest, and that if on a slope, the head is lower than the feet.

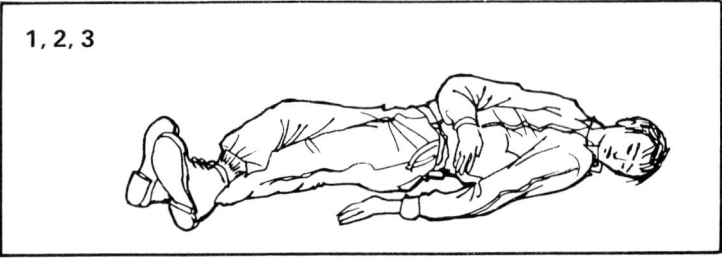

1, 2, 3

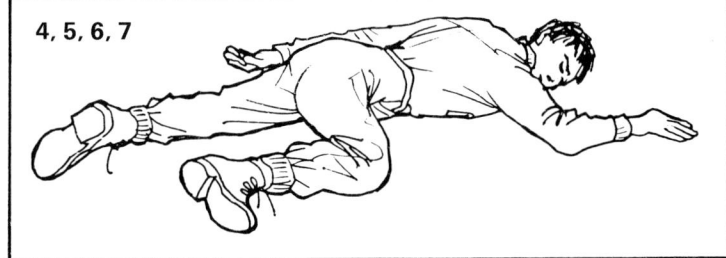

4, 5, 6, 7

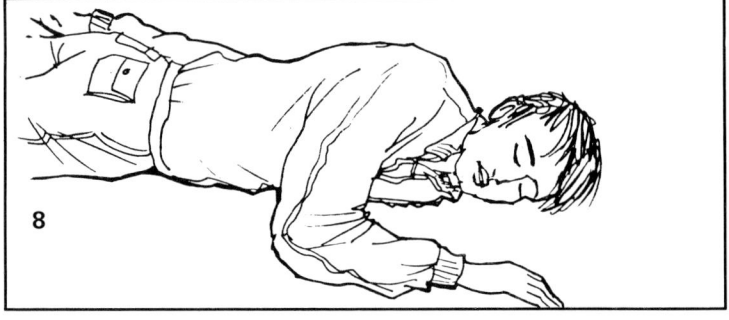

8

Less-serious injuries

If the accident does not result in a 'life or death' situation, then the consciousness test and the ABC procedure can be omitted. There follows general guidelines on what to do for some of the less-serious types of injury you are likely to come across some time or other. These injuries could happen either to yourself, a member of your party or someone you meet when outside. Your teacher/instructor will arrange plenty of practical exercises in bandaging and treatment, so that you are thoroughly familiar with these procedures.

The most common minor injury is the **blister**. This is a burn of the skin caused by rubbing. The immediate treatment is simply to add an artificial layer of 'skin' over the blister—i.e. apply a sterile plaster.

For other types of **burns** or **scalds** you should pour on cold water or fully-immerse the part of the body affected in cold water for at least ten minutes. If no running or clean water is available, then any cold liquid, e.g. milk, can be used to cool the burn. After cooling, the burn should be covered with sterile dressings to keep the air out. Never put cream or ointment on burns or scalds.

Shock symptoms should be expected with burns, as well as with other accidents. Shock can easily turn a minor injury into a serious situation. The clues for shock are a pale face, sweating and shivering. Before dealing with the initial injury, get the casualty to sit or lie down. Keep them warm and reassure them constantly with cheerful conversation, whilst waiting for help.

Mild bleeding can be stopped as described in the ABC procedure, by applying pressure which allows clotting to occur. Clean the area around the cut and cover it with a sterile dressing. It is important when washing the wound to use *clean* cotton wool and to work *outwards* from the cut, so that there is no risk of moving grit and dirt into the injured area.

Nose bleed is quite common; the treatment is to squeeze the lower part of the nose (below the bone) between the finger and thumb for about ten minutes. Do not lean back or lie down on your back.

Broken bones and **dislocations** are extremely painful. Never try to replace broken bones into their correct positions—this is a job for experts only. Clues which suggest a broken bone include shock, swelling and a deformity (i.e. part of the body appears the wrong shape/in the wrong position). If you are not sure, then always assume that there *is* a fracture or dislocation. If the casualty is able to walk to safety, the injury should be immobilised, i.e. the area should be supported in order to keep it still. This can be done by bandaging the affected area to uninjured parts of the body. Bandage firmly but not too tightly, and apply padding beneath the bandage for comfort. If you are unsure about moving a limb in order to immobilise it, then don't: make the casualty safe and get help instead.

Strains (pulled muscles) and **sprains** (pulled ligaments—the structures that help to hold bones together) can be dealt with by applying cold compresses in order to reduce the swelling. (However, do not apply cold compresses if the casualty is showing signs of hypothermia too.) The joint should then be supported by applying cotton wool and firm (not tight) bandages.

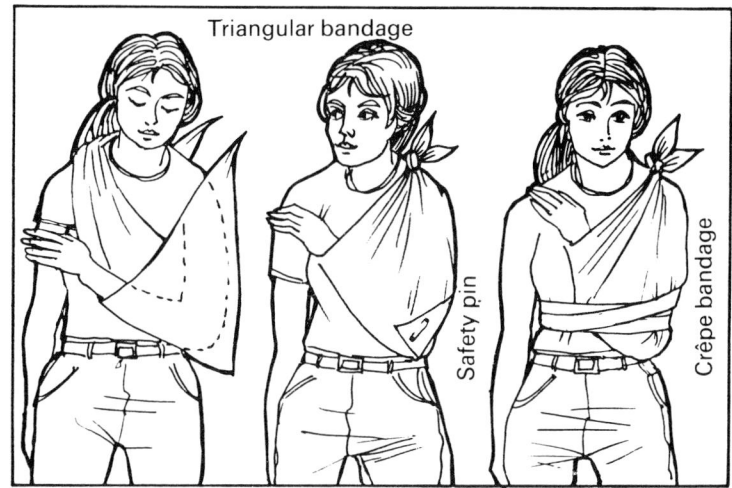

Applying a triangular bandage

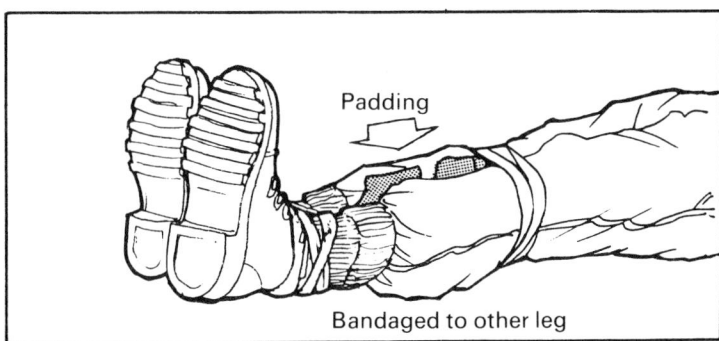

With suspected broken bones, bandage firmly and use plenty padding

Muscle cramp is a common complaint. It should be dealt with by stopping the activity and stretching the affected muscle.

A first-aid kit for a small outdoor pursuits group should include the following items:
1. six sterile adhesive dressings
2. four sterile unmedicated dressings
3. six triangular bandages
4. selection of crêpe bandages
5. zinc oxide sticking plaster or tape
6. safety pins
7. packet of assorted plasters
8. absorbent, sterilised cotton wool
9. scissors
10. some tablets for pain relief (e.g. Paracetamol)
11. mouthpiece (Portex barrier type)
12. surgical gloves (protection pack)

The larger the group, the more first-aid equipment needs to be taken. In any situation, effective first aid means being prepared, and knowing what action to take.

Further information

The associations listed below will be pleased to supply further information on basic first-aid/training schemes, etc.

The St John Ambulance Association and Brigade
The St Andrews Ambulance Association
The British Red Cross

Look in the telephone book for your local branch or group.

If your concern is for water safety, you should find out about the Royal Life Saving Society's Water Safety Award. The national office is at:
Royal Life Saving Society
Mountbatten House
Studley
Warwickshire
B80 7NN

APPENDIX B: THE COUNTRYSIDE AND CONSERVATION

Outdoor pursuits can take place almost anywhere, but although much work has recently been done to develop activities within cities, the most important area to us remains the countryside.

What is the countryside?

The countryside can be simply defined as land outwith a town or city. It is often described as the most important leisure resource we have because it allows us to take part in all kinds of activities, from just enjoying the peace and quiet, the sights and the smells, to total survival and dependence upon the living environment.

But the countryside is also a **shared resource**. All land belongs to someone, and the owners and users of countryside may find that their interests sometimes conflict. Over-use of natural areas can spoil them for ever, depriving future generations of the enjoyment these places can offer if treated carefully. It is possible to use the countryside for recreation without doing it any harm at all. In fact, it is our responsibility to make sure that our activities do not cause damage.

When taking part in outdoor pursuits, we must learn to look after this most valuable asset and to help others to do so as well. In other words, we must learn how to conserve the countryside.

THE COUNTRYSIDE

How can we help to conserve it?

Everyone who uses the countryside should be concerned about looking after it and making sure that it remains the way it is for others to enjoy. This is what conservation means. But how can we conserve the countryside? Unless we know how to use it properly, we might do the wrong things. Our outdoor pursuits activities can easily damage the land and wildlife, so we must always be careful. Following **the country code** is therefore very important.

The country code

1. Enjoy the countryside and respect its life and work.
2. Guard against all risks of fire.
3. Fasten all gates.
4. Keep your dog under control.
5. Keep to public paths across farmland.
6. Use gates and stiles to cross fences and walls—don't climb.
7. Leave livestock, crops and machinery alone.
8. Take your litter home.
9. Help to keep all water clean.
10. Protect the wildlife, plants and trees.
11. Take special care on country roads.
12. Make no unnecessary noise.

Further information

For more information on how to look after the countryside, addresses of National Park offices and places to stay, here are some contacts. Remember: Look after the countryside—it's the only one we've got!

If you would like to find out more about how to get involved in practical conservation work write to:

British Trust for Conservation Volunteers (BTCV), 10–14 Duke Street, Reading, Berkshire RG1 4RU. Tel: 0734 596171

For Scotland write to: BTCV, 70 Main Street, Doune, Perthshire FK16 6BW. Tel: 0786 84479

Here are just a few countryside bodies. They will provide information on National Parks and other special places.

Countryside Commission, John Dower House, Crescent Place, Cheltenham, Glos GL50 3RA. Tel: 0242 21381

The Forestry Commission, 231 Corstorphine Road, Edinburgh EH12 7AT. Tel: 031 334 0303

The National Trust, 42 Queen Anne's Gate, London SW1H 9AH. Tel: 01 222 9251

The National Trust for Scotland, 5 Charlotte Square, Edinburgh EH2 4DU. Tel: 031 226 5922

Nature Conservancy Council, 19/20 Belgrave Square, London SW1X 8PY. Tel: 01 235 3241

To get information on where to stay and courses on offer, the following addresses will be useful.

Youth Hostel Association (YHA), Trevelyan House, 8 St Stephens Hill, St Albans, Herts. AL1 2DY. Tel: 0727 55215

The Outward Bound Trust, Chestnut Field, Regent Place, Rugby CU21 2PS. Tel: 0788 60423/4/5

The Outward Bound Trust have a video available which explains the various courses on offer.

INDEX

A
ABC technique 138
abseiling 100
access 111
accidents 35
alpine distress signal 41
anoraks 28
attack point 73

B
backing 97
backpacking 44
base camp 44
bearing 14, 15, 18
belaying 84, 94, 99
belts 84
bivouac 37
bleeding 141
blister 140
boots 29, 93
bouldering 88
bow rescue 128
breeches 83
bridging 97
broken bones 141
buoyancy 115, 119

C
cagoules 28
camping 52
   equipment 44
Canadian canoe 108
capsizing 121
carrying methods 38
catching feature 73
chimney 86, 97
classic abseil 100
climbing
   calls 94
   cracks 96
   equipment 89
   grades 87
   onto a ledge 96
code 78
compass 12, 13
contour 9, 11
country code 143
courses (orienteering) 78
crack 86
cramp 142

D
day sack 30
deep water skills 127
   rescue 129
depressions 58, 69

descendeur 100
description sheet 76
double buckling 92
draw stroke 126
driprings 120
dry suit 118

E
escape routes 34
expeditions 56

F
feathering 120
features 11, 86
fibre-glass 110
first-aid 138
fly sheet 45
food 56
footholds 84
footrest 115
forward sweep 124
fronts 58

G
gas stoves 49
gate 92, 113
grid lines/references 9
   north 15
gulley 86

H
harness 91, 100
Hawser-laid 90
hazards 58
height 10
helmet 92, 118
high 58
hip
   belay 99
   flick 132
hypothermia 39

I
inner clothes 27
isobars 58

J
jamming 86, 96

K
karabiners 84, 91
kayak 108, 109
keel 116
kernmantel 90
Klets sole 29
knots 98

L
layback 96
ledge 86
life-jacket 119
line features 72
long distance walks 60
low 59
   brace turn 125

M
magnetic
   north 15, 68
   pole 12
mantelshelfing 96
map
   measure 32
   scale 7
   'setting' 12, 16
   signs 9
   master 77
meths stove 50

N
Naismith's rule 32
north points 16

O
orienteering map 67
outer clothes 28
overhang 86

P
pace 23
pacing 74
paddle 120
   strokes 123
paraffin stoves 49
Pawlata 131, 133
pre-start 77
Primus stove 49
'push' support stroke 131

R
rescues 128
resource 142
reverse sweep 125
rock
   face 85
   features 86
   skills 82
   steepness 85
rolling 131
rope 84, 89, 100
route
   card 31, 35
   choice 32, 72

length 32
planning 31
rucksack 30, 50

S
scale 7
scrambling 26
scree 25, 26
screw roll 131, 135
'setting' (a map) 12, 16
shock 141
Silva compass 13
slalom 109
sleeping bag 47
sling 101
spray cover 121, 127
Sticht plate 99
stonefly 55
stove 48
strain 141
stream 27
striking camp 56
support strokes 130
survival bag 37
sweep turn 124
swimmer-to-canoeist
   rescue 128

T
tents 45, 54
terrain 25
thumbing 70
toggles 115
top rope belay 94
Trangia stove 50
troll 91
turning strokes 124
'TX' method 130

U
unconsciousness 140
undulating 11

V
Vango tent 46
Vibram sole 29

W
waistbelt 91
walls 84, 85
weather 58
Weil's disease 135
wet suit 118

X
'X' method 129